Authentic Project-Based Learning in Grades 4–8

Authentic Project-Based Learning in Grades 4–8 provides a clear guide to design, develop, and implement real-world challenges for any middle school subject. The author lays out five clear, standards-based stages of assessment to help you and your learners process the what, how, and why of authentic project-based experiences.

You'll learn how to create projects that:

- Align with your content standards
- Integrate technology effectively
- Support reading and writing development
- Utilize formative assessment
- Allow for multiple complex pathways to emerge
- Facilitate the development of essential skills beyond school

Each chapter includes a variety of practical examples to assist with scaffolding and implementation. The templates and tools in the appendix are also provided on our website as free eResources for ease of use.

Dayna Laur (@daylynn) is the co-founder of Project ARC, an educational consulting organization that promotes the development of authentic, relevant, and complex learning experiences. Dayna leads workshops on project-based learning (PBL), authentic learning experiences, inquiry learning, critical thinking, Advanced Placement, technology integration, 1:1 programs, and STEAM. She trains nationally, internationally, and through online support. She is the author of two prior Routledge publications and is currently completing her dissertation in Instructional Systems Design and Technology.

Also Available from Routledge Eye On Education
(www.routledge.com/k-12)

Authentic Project-Based Learning in Grades 9–12:
Standards-Based Strategies and Scaffolding for Success
Dayna Laur

Developing Natural Curiosity through Project-Based Learning:
Five Strategies for the PreK-3 Classroom
Dayna Laur and Jill Ackers

Creating Citizens:
Teaching Civics and Current Events in the History Classroom, 6-9
Sarah Cooper

The Genius Hour Guidebook:
Fostering Passion, Wonder, and Inquiry in the Classroom
Denise Krebs and Gallit Zvi

STEM by Design:
Strategies and Activities for Grades 4-8
Anne Jolly

The Flexible ELA Classroom:
Practical Tools for Differentiated Instruction in Grades 4-8
Amber Chandler

It's a Matter of Fact:
Teaching Students Research Skills in Today's Information-Packed World
Angie Miller

Working Hard, Working Happy:
Cultivating a Culture of Effort and Joy in the Classroom
Rita Platt

Authentic Project-Based Learning in Grades 4–8

Standards-Based Strategies and Scaffolding for Success

Dayna Laur

Routledge
Taylor & Francis Group
NEW YORK AND LONDON

First published 2020
by Routledge
52 Vanderbilt Avenue, New York, NY 10017

and by Routledge
2 Park Square, Milton Park, Abingdon, Oxon, OX14 4RN

Routledge is an imprint of the Taylor & Francis Group, an informa business

© 2020 Taylor & Francis

The right of Dayna Laur to be identified as author of this work has been asserted by her in accordance with sections 77 and 78 of the Copyright, Designs and Patents Act 1988.

All rights reserved. No part of this book may be reprinted or reproduced or utilised in any form or by any electronic, mechanical, or other means, now known or hereafter invented, including photocopying and recording, or in any information storage or retrieval system, without permission in writing from the publishers.

Trademark notice: Product or corporate names may be trademarks or registered trademarks, and are used only for identification and explanation without intent to infringe.

Library of Congress Cataloging-in-Publication Data
Names: Laur, Dayna, author.
Title: Authentic project-based learning in 9-12 : standards-based strategies and scaffolding for success / Dayna Laur.
Description: New York, NY : Routledge, 2020. | Includes bibliographical references.
Identifiers: LCCN 2019020368 (print) | LCCN 2019022376 (ebook) | ISBN 9780367225100 (hardback) | ISBN 9780367225117 (pbk.) | ISBN 9780429275258 (ebk)
Subjects: LCSH: Project method in teaching. | Education, Secondary–Curricula. | Academic achievement.
Classification: LCC LB1027.43 .L384 2020 (print) | LCC LB1027.43 (ebook) | DDC 373.01/1–dc23
LC record available at https://lccn.loc.gov/2019020368
LC ebook record available at https://lccn.loc.gov/2019022376

ISBN: 978-0-367-22508-7 (hbk)
ISBN: 978-0-367-22509-4 (pbk)
ISBN: 978-0-429-27524-1 (ebk)

Typeset in Palatino
by Swales & Willis, Exeter, Devon, UK

Visit the eResources: www.routledge.com/9780367225094

Contents

eResources vi
Meet the Author vii
Acknowledgments viii

1 Authentic Concept Creation 1

2 Align Content Standards to the Real World 13

3 Support Digital Transformation 35

4 Generate Authentic Reading and Writing 50

5 Formative Assessments for Success 70

6 Levels of Complexity 85

7 Essential Skills for Tomorrow 101

8 Commonly Asked Questions about PBL 123

Appendix 1: A Guide to Tools, Activities, and Protocols 134
Appendix 2: Templates and Tools 146
Appendix 3: Suggested Options for Authentic Challenge Questions 148
Bibliography 149

eResources

The templates in Appendix 2 can also be downloaded and printed for ease of use. You can access these downloads by visiting the book product page on our website: www.routledge.com/9780367225094. Then click on the tab that says "eResources," and select the files. They will begin downloading to your computer.

Meet the Author

Dayna Laur (@daylynn) is a veteran social studies teacher for multiple grade levels and courses. She has extensive co-teaching experience in a special education setting and has worked as a Career Academy Coordinator for the Health Sciences and Human Services sector. Dayna holds a B.A. in History from Virginia Tech, an M.Ed. in Curriculum and Instruction from the University of Pittsburgh, and an M.S. in 21st Century Teaching and Learning from Wilkes University. She is a two-time National Board Certified teacher. Currently, she is ABD as she completes her dissertation in Instructional Systems Design and Technology at Sam Houston State University.

Dayna is the co-founder of Project ARC where she works with districts and technology companies to transform best educational practices into more authentic, relevant, and appropriately complex learning experiences. Through this work, both stateside and internationally, Dayna strives to empower educators and their learners by implementing authentic challenges, a topic she pioneered in her 2013 Routledge book, *Authentic Learning Experiences: A Real-World Approach to Project-Based Learning*.

Acknowledgments

Writing a book takes considerable time, effort, and commitment. Inevitably, when an author signs on to pursue the challenge that comes with writing, personal and professional areas of life suffer in some regards. Consequently, every experienced author knows that a well-written book means they had an excellent support system of family, friends, and editors who guided the way. Thankfully, I have an encouraging network that steps up every time I decide to tackle a new book.

My wonderful husband and best friend, Eric, put up with the glow of my computer screen and the clacking of keys for many nights, as I wrote in bed for an hour or two after he turned off the lights. My daughters, Claire and Lydia, cheered me on while I wrote and never complained when I occasionally declined a family outing so that I could finish a chapter. My business partner and dear friend, Tim Kubik, was frequently a sounding board, as I ran ideas past him on more than a few occasions, and he provided me with valuable feedback to enhance my thinking. My co-author on our earlier PreK-3 PBL book, Jill Ackers, helped to develop the original ideas for the Five Stages of Finding a Solution from which the Stages of Assessment in this book were refined and deepened. Jill also initially collaborated on preliminary discussions regarding the first chapter of this book and provided some feedback for Chapter 2. I am fortunate to watch her now fill the critical role of enriching the lives of global teachers as she focuses on the architecture of designing learning spaces. My editor, Lauren Davis, with whom I reunited for these books, supported me throughout the journey of writing them. Her encouragement and expertise are unparalleled, and I am eternally grateful for her guidance. To all of the teachers whom I featured in this book, thank you for your unwavering dedication to your learners as they discover their potential and define their stories of authentic, relevant, and complex learning.

1

Authentic Concept Creation

> How do we empower our learners to potentially effect change in their communities?

An Introduction

A friend of mine and author of *Faces of Learning: 50 Powerful Stories of Defining Moments in Education*, Sam Chaltain, spent a significant chunk of time asking people to recall their most memorable learning experience. When I met Sam in 2011, and he asked me this question, I had a difficult time responding. You see, my educational story reads like this: I was the student who followed the rules, checked the boxes, and easily played the game of school. However, I was bored. Here's exactly what I remember from late elementary, middle school, and very early high school, as my school district was so small that eighth grade was part of the high school!

- In the fourth grade, I failed my first and only test. I was a terrible speller, but I was good at memorizing. I was also very tall, so I sat at the back of the class. I copied my spelling words from the board, memorized them, took the test, and missed every single one. It turned out I needed glasses.

- In the fifth grade, I tried kiwi for the first time as part of a special celebration. I can't recall what that celebration was all about.
- In the sixth grade, I made, or rather my mom made, a rice crispy treat pyramid to show what I "learned" about ancient Egypt.
- In the seventh grade, I earned the "gifted" label. All this netted me was the right to complete a lot of extra worksheets for "enrichment."
- In the eighth grade, I was the only person who knew all three rivers that met at the confluence of Pittsburgh for the geography bee.

Unfortunately, I see a similarly defined path with my youngest daughter who is currently in the fifth grade. Apparently, the apple doesn't fall far from the tree. While she is in the advanced class for all of her subjects and is in the "special interest" class for gifted students, she is bored. School, for her, is just a job. She goes to school to see her friends and for playing her violin, participating in physical education class, representing her peers on the student council, and being a bus monitor. While she is categorically disengaged with the learning process, I feel fortunate that she is a "good" kid who wouldn't dream of being a class disruption. However, I don't want her current experience to define her educational story.

To shift the learning experience ecosystem into one that allows learners to write their educational story and define their educational journey, we must invert how we have traditionally approached lesson planning. Rather than start from a bottom-up strategy, we should move to a top-down design. This top-down design is one that immediately asks our learners to start with a challenge rather than begin with the basics. (Stick with me here and don't put this book down yet!)

Conventional projects as you know them, and more than likely project-based learning as you have heard it explained in general terms, are not what allow our learners to write their educational story. These conventional projects happen at the end of a unit and come with a host of guidelines that we require our learners to check off, one by one, to develop an end product that meets our predetermined notion of what is considered proficient or advanced. All of the "learning" takes place ahead of the project. Lessons, activities, readings, and often a test lead up to the project implementation. The project aligns to the previously taught unit to ensure our learners know what they need to do. Sometimes, this project is in lieu of a test, or it might be an attempt to enhance the grades of those that don't test well.

While included as an integral part of the title of this book, project-based learning as it is generally defined and explained is not what you will explore as you turn these pages. You can throw out all of your old notions of PBL that ask learners to complete a task that is then shared at a local exhibition night and comes with tri-fold poster boards for parents to "ooh" and "aah" over. These projects start with an entry event meant to engage students and a need-to-know list that is supposed to begin the process of inquiry that emerges from a driving question – for a list of these driving questions, check out Table 1.1. They are a random but not exhaustive list that I compiled from a quick Google search. As you review each of these questions, consider the differences between the listed driving question and the authentic challenge ideas reviewed in Table 1.4 later in this chapter. As the pages of this book unfold, I intend to challenge the conventional notion of PBL, which lacks many of the fundamental attributes of an authentic learning experience that is instead a call for participation to potentially effect change in the world.

As you begin to consider the shortcomings of traditionally written driving questions, you should recognize that these sample questions are written at a low-level of Bloom's Taxonomy. One of the goals for me in writing this book is to help you understand the differences between conventionally designed project-based learning and truly authentic challenges that I believe have somehow gotten lost in much of the current PBL vernacular. To facilitate our learners as they self-direct their educational story and choose the pathway of their educational journey, we must provide them with the open-ended possibilities that come with an authentic, relevant, and complex challenge. These questions now shift from low-level Bloom's to a high-level, "How can we (I) ...?" The use of this question stem creates multiple possibilities for solutions, is actionable, and puts our learners in charge of their educational story. And, I promise our pre-teens and teens are ready to tackle these challenges even before we "teach" them everything we think they need to know.

At this age, it is imperative that we pique the interest of our learners through the exciting challenges that an authentic learning experience affords them. Too frequently, we shelter our learners from the trials of the

Table 1.1 Driving Questions

Driving Questions
What is epic poetry?
Can we trust our government?
Is the water in our town safe to drink?
What effect does population growth have on our community?
How is geometry reflected in art?

real world, as we fear they are too inexperienced and don't have the skills or knowledge to delve into the problems that we, as grown-ups, try to solve. However, our upper elementary and middle school learners are full of questions and have become more independent in finding the answers to them. Instead of a primary focus on the preparation for what we imagine the future requires of our learners, we must remember that our learners are active participants in the real world. In the words of my colleague and friend Tim Kubik, "participation is preparation." Thus, it is our job to encourage our learners as they define their educational story and begin to make impactful changes before they ever leave our halls and classrooms.

How do we empower our learners to potentially effect change in their communities? By the age of ten or eleven, our kids are starting to take on more responsibilities at home. By the age of twelve, many kids have started to babysit for other children, if they haven't already been tasked with taking care of younger siblings. It also isn't inconceivable for some of our middle school children to take on neighborhood jobs. At the same time, organized athletics become more important, as some may join a travel team, and by seventh grade our schools officially compete in many sports. These responsibilities give our adolescents a taste of freedom and the desire to move beyond what many traditional classrooms have to offer them. Think about the number of learners who enter your class daily and are distracted by the world outside of school. They are eager to delve into meaningful work that exposes them to the world beyond the confines of the textbook and scripted units we may offer.

While we might not understand their constant need to communicate socially via Houseparty or Snapchat, we can connect to their desire for relevancy. If we consider all of the times we have been required to sit through a professional development session that struggled to hold our attention, we have a baseline for understanding our learners. Thus, it is our responsibility to create and co-develop with them a classroom ecosystem that is relevant to their lives, while enhancing their essential skills and solidifying their understanding of complex content.

This classroom ecosystem offers an opportunity to investigate a complex as opposed to complicated challenge where our learners develop new ideas rather than produce what we believe is the right answer. If we invite our learners to participate in real-life challenges in place of a required assignment, we allow our students to become agile learners ready to explore and discover, as they initiate their learning through the process of inquiry inherently required in an open-ended challenge. Through an open-ended challenge, our learners have the occasion to develop an entirely new set of attributes that many pre-teens and teens are accused of lacking (Table 1.2). More importantly, as we design and co-design, with our learners and technical experts, authentic learning opportunities that are relevant to our learners and their communities, we empower them to effect positive change beyond simply giving back in the form of community service.

I promise this book isn't about how I want you to abandon all of your current classroom practices. Instead, I want you to think about how you can level up your pedagogical approaches. There is no need to start from scratch. Don't throw away all your lesson plans, as these are often good scaffolds for supporting your learners in their project challenges; although, I won't complain if you toss out your worksheets and packets! The most successful authentic learning experiences are grounded in the best instructional practices. Moreover, please note that I use various terms interchangeably throughout this book. "Authentic learning experiences" is an umbrella term that I use, but I know districts have adopted "project-based learning," "inquiry learning," "authentic challenges," and other similar phrases to describe their focus on a more open-ended, inquiry-driven approach to education. Therefore, I, too, use a variety of terms to describe the work in this book.

As we begin to dive into our content, remember this first chapter is merely meant to be an introduction to this pedagogical shift in your educational story; think of it as the 30,000-foot view. If you find yourself asking questions, that's a good thing! Asking questions is part of the inquiry process, and you are the learner in this process. I promise we will go into much greater detail in the chapters to come.

As we start to consider the development of authentic project-based learning experiences, we move beyond complicated activities that have a right answer according to the teacher's guide or the department committee that crafted the activity. These authentic challenges are much more than a community service project. Now, we focus our content and standards in an authentic and relevant context. In turn, our learners become agile and responsive learners who can adapt to the challenge based on this context rather than simply the content. More importantly, our learners have shifted from the application of complicated concepts via a single lesson to the integration of a unit of lessons targeted toward the creation of complex

Table 1.2 Learner Attributes Developed Through Authentic Challenges

Agility	Initiative
Awareness	Imaginative
Curiosity	Motivation
Collaborative	Observant
Flexibility	Self-advocacy

solutions to open-ended challenges. Our newly independent learners can now determine what pathway to explore as they seek possible ideas for an end-user. It is especially critical for us to foster this autonomy, as our learners, by grade four, are developmentally ready for more independence even though they are clearly still children. By middle school, our learners are straddling the line between child and young adult. Our decisions on how to balance independence and support are vital in the development of our learners as independent thinkers. Therefore, by understanding the needs of our learners, we design for exploration on multiple levels.

With learner autonomy, our role now shifts to that of a facilitator as we encourage self-discovery of information through the inquiry process but also scaffold knowledge acquisition through protocols, activities, and mini-lessons. As we complete formative assessments throughout the learning process, we may experience the need to support one or more learners directly. This guidance ensures our learners have not stumbled into frustration due to a lack of understanding or confusion. Here, a more traditional lesson plan may be appropriate as long as it does not happen before you introduce the challenge. Otherwise, we end up with just another project!

As we shift from a teaching/modeling first mentality to one of learner exploration with guided help as needed, we must rely more heavily on Bloom's Taxonomy than ever before. Based on our formative assessment outcomes, we may need to support one, some, or all of our learners at the lower levels of Bloom's. However, these lower levels are not where you begin. As you will discover throughout this book, it is necessary to write your challenge at the creation or highest level of Bloom's. From here, the process of inquiry gets underway, and now a learner-led guide provides information on how to help our learners, when needed, through the more basic levels of Bloom's.

To review this concept, compare the question stems from the lowest three levels of Bloom's to the highest three levels of Bloom's in Table 1.3. These question stems scaffold our learners to be able to reach the pinnacle of higher order thinking. Now, we replace what I like to call a research paper in disguise with a novel solution to a challenge that, in reality, has no single right answer. Conclusively, we have a clearer vision of our learners' deep understanding of the content and standards, as memorization of information necessitates no critical thinking, while open-ended challenges, in contrast, automatically require the deepest levels of thinking. Perhaps this is why my educational story from fourth to eighth grade is so shallow. Feel free to use the questions from Table 1.3 as a guide to scaffold your learners in their quest to devise a feasible solution for the given challenge.

Table 1.3 Scaffolded Questions via the Lens of Bloom's

Bloom's Taxonomy	Question
Creating	How can you reimagine the current solution in a better way? If you had one dollar, how would you solve the challenge? If you had one million dollars, how would you solve the challenge?
Evaluating	How well does the solution for the challenge work for a neighboring community? What are the downsides to this claim? How well did the solution for the challenge work in the past?
Analyzing	How does the evidence relate to your views? What is a counter example of the proposed solution? How would you categorize the proposed solutions as new, useful, and feasible?
Applying	How can you select the most appropriate resources to help you solve the challenge? What element could you introduce to change the problem? How does this problem change if we change one element?
Understanding	How is this idea consistent across time? How are "x" and "y" connected? How can you illustrate the given problem?
Remembering	What is the problem? How did the problem start? What are the major elements of the problem?

When we frame a unit in the context of a project challenge, all of our lessons, scaffolded through activities, readings, and protocols, push our learners to deepen their thinking. As their thinking is extended, new questions emerge as our learners engage in the process of inquiry. This inquiry process is sometimes a new phenomenon for our older learners.

At the later elementary grades and middle school level, while our learners may sometimes beg for the "one right answer" to make the grade, especially at the seventh- and eighth-grade years, they also enjoy the process of innovation. Innovation is supported through inquiry. Inquiry, at this level, is dependent on each learner, and requires us to scaffold the process for our classes. The sample questions in Table 1.3 are effective as part of those scaffolds. Some of our learners are ready to jump into inquiry, while for others the guided exploration that results from Table 1.3 may be necessary. Although, we must also be careful to ensure we don't lead our learners down the path we perceive as the correct one.

Authentic challenges are a learning journey. Therefore, we have to be comfortable with not knowing exactly what our learners will produce as the solution to the challenge. However, just as an expert in the world outside of education works with clients who require a specific product, we may also decide to request a particular format for an end product. For example, we might require a prototype diagram or a detailed budget. However, we do not want to tell our learners what that prototype diagram or detailed budget will ultimately look like as the summative product. Ten different prototype diagram submissions should look very different from one another.

The Value of Community Partnerships

Traditional projects are easily found online, passed down from veteran teachers, or are relics of our own schooling experience. Authentic learning experiences, on the other hand, require an intentional and concerted effort to link our content and standards with the real world in a relevant context for our learners. We focus more on our standards connection in the next chapter. For now, the three components to keep in mind are authenticity, relevancy, and complexity. These components comprise the framework of the work that we do at Project ARC. Authenticity requires a link to the world beyond the classroom in the form of a community or a career connection and was the focus of my first book, *Authentic Learning Experiences: A Real-World Approach to Project-Based Learning* (2013). Relevancy links the authentic work to that which matters to our learners. It doesn't matter how real it is; if our learners don't understand how it personally has an impact on them, they won't care beyond getting a good grade on an assignment. Finally, the complexity of the challenge must allow for multiple pathways to emerge in their learning through inquiry. A complex problem is dynamic and multi-dimensional and could produce any number of learner solutions.

As you consider promising community connections for your project, let's begin with potential ideas that you can envision as possible challenges within your curriculum. For this, you may have to think outside the box and ditch your scope and sequence viewpoint. Trust me, it will work, and if you still have more questions than answers right now, that's okay, too. If you are just starting out, you will likely be the only one designing the challenge. However, as you become more experienced in this process, co-designing with teachers from other content areas becomes appealing. And, I highly encourage you to explore co-designing with technical experts once you feel more confident. If you are open to it, there is even the possibility that your learners can initiate the challenge!

As we design an open-ended problem it is also critical to tap into the relevancy of our learners' everyday experiences. It doesn't matter how authentic or real-world the problem is, if our learners don't comprehend how the challenge connects to them, we may lose them from the start. Since our learners, at this age, have limited experiences, we must figure out how to create new experiences that will foster a relevant connection to their lives. To foster these new experiences, we can develop partnerships in an authentic learning experience to nurture the connection between our learners and locally available community assets.

All communities have assets unique to their location. The trick is to figure out how these assets connect to your curriculum, and in turn, how they can connect to the development of your authentic challenge. These organizations, businesses, and government agencies have technical experts who have the real-world experience that your learners could benefit from as they engage in the challenge. In fact, you can turn to these assets to help you and your learners co-develop the challenge. In doing so, you automatically create an authentic experience for your learners. This experience becomes a relevant one when your technical experts and community assets engage your learners as the new perspective they need to help solve a problem with which they have struggled.

You should also consider any problems your community faces; each community has relevant problems that connect to a variety of subject areas. These problems are the potential for your learners to actively engage in a relevant issue to effect positive change as mentioned at the start of this chapter. The possibilities are endless and unique to your back yard, and you should never fret over how small or large your community might seem to you. Even the smallest towns I have worked in (think one paved road and fewer than 500 residents) offer the potential to attack relevant issues such as the overpopulation of stray dogs and cats roaming freely, while a large suburban area may suffer from a lack of green space for pet owners to exercise their dogs. Both areas, while vastly different from one another, have commonalities in their challenges. However, the context of this challenge requires a very different approach for a feasible solution. Thus, we wouldn't want to ask members of one community to solve the problem of another since the context isn't relevant to them. Table 1.4 provides additional inspiration on community-based project ideas that you can tailor to your relevant needs and to the content area you teach, as each of these ideas can easily incorporate social studies, science, math, ELA, and some of our specials. And, if you are missing one of these organizations in your community, start to think about virtual connections that may be an alternative.

As our learners and technical experts develop a networked relationship, this creates a public relations opportunity between our schools and our community. As we forge this partnership, we also open the door to possible internships, scholarships, and donorships. Don't, however, overlook the potential that exists

Table 1.4 Community-Based Project Ideas

Community Assets	General Project Ideas to Tailor to Your Audience
Airport	Craft a plan to make aviation of the future safer in the wake of the Boeing crisis
	Devise a proposal to bring more air routes/airlines to the region
Chamber of Commerce	Develop an economic plan for the business future of the region
	Redevelop a use for an abandoned property
Conservation District	Design a plan for the conservation of farmland
	Create a proposal to conserve water resources while efficiently irrigating crops
Department of Transportation	Redesign the traffic patterns for a pedestrian and auto-heavy intersection
	Develop a public transportation system suitable to the size of the community in an effort to decrease automobile traffic
Public Library	Design an app to provide virtual services to the community while keeping the physical space relevant
	Create a plan to increase government funding for the library

to create a bond between our learners and community partnerships that foster the inquiry process with them. Often, teachers and outreach organizations view the use of technical experts in the classroom as relegated to merely report information about the community or their jobs. Instead, we want to use our technical experts as true assets in the learning process, as they can co-design challenges, provide a differing perspective to the challenge, and provide valuable insight in the form of feedback as our learners develop and refine their ideas as solutions to a given problem.

Five Project Assessment Stages

Every one of us, no matter what challenge we may face, goes through a process to resolve that challenge. The challenge may be as small as figuring out how to adapt a recipe when we are missing an ingredient or two, or the challenge may be as complex as redesigning our house to make it handicap accessible for an elderly loved one who we have invited into our home. While we have spent a lot of time talking about the need to make the challenge authentic and relevant to our learners, the challenge itself is only part of the picture.

Here, I share with you a series of five stages that you will repeatedly encounter throughout the rest of this book. These stages, initially designed by Jill Ackers, my co-author on a previous PreK-3 book, and myself, were meant to describe the process that learners engage in as they solve challenges. However, since the publication of that book in 2017, I have spent a lot of time revising the stages with the help of my Project ARC partner, Tim Kubik. At Project ARC, we utilize this version of the stages that I share here. For quite some time now, as we partner with districts and businesses from a variety of locations, we have devised a unique process to support teachers, learners, and technical experts as they co-create meaning out of the challenges they tackle. Through those invaluable partnerships, we have realized these stages are assessment-focused rather than design stages. Thus, the stages serve as double duty for your purposes. In your learners' quests to uncover new ideas, these five stages are a way for you to chart the inquiry process, gather evidence, and provide feedback to your learners as they transition from stage to stage. However, these stages also help you to process the what, how, and why of authentic project-based experiences in a visual and concrete manner. As you become more familiar with these stages, please note that they are not linear. As you assess your learners in each stage, you will find the need to sometimes circle back to a stage with one, some, or all of your learners.

I have aligned the Five Stages of Project Assessment to critical questions that will assist you in your assessment of your learners' thinking throughout the implementation of the project (Table 1.5). As you design your challenge, these questions will help you predict what might occur at each stage of the project. These questions will also serve to help you assess your learners as you establish whether or not they are ready to move on to the next stage or if they need to revisit an earlier stage.

As I promised, the remainder of this book will take you through the process of designing an authentic, relevant, and appropriately complex learning experience for your classroom. It is my sincere hope that you will shift from mere projects to more meaningful learning experiences worthy of sharing

Table 1.5 Guiding Questions for Assessment

Project Stage	Question
Stage One: Challenge and Purpose	How do we know if our learners understand and are invested in the challenge?
Stage Two: Inquiry and Ideas	How do we know if our learners have explored multiple pathways to a solution?
Stage Three: Context and Perspective	How do we know if our learners have considered end-user needs and technical expert feedback?
Stage Four: Actions and Consequences	How do we know if our learners have considered potential positive and negative impacts of their solution?
Stage Five: Options and Opportunities	How do we know if our learners have developed an actionable solution for their end-users?

with Sam Chaltain. Know that this journey isn't one that happens overnight. Instead, you will experience the ups and downs that inevitably come with change. Know that I, too, have been there! I have had crying pre-teens frustrated over inaction, but I have also experienced, first-hand, the joy that spreads when change does occur. That is what motivated me to continue this writing journey and share the stories of my learners and those from many excellent teachers I've met along the way; I couldn't have done this without them. As you read through the remainder of this book, use these guiding questions to reflect on your learning. Please don't skip this critical step in your journey. Feel free to write in this book directly or use post-it notes if you prefer.

Time to Reflect
1. What community resources and technical experts do you have available that may help you co-design an authentic challenge?
2. How do your content and standards specifically relate to these assets?
3. How will using these resources make your class more authentic, relevant, and complex than your traditional approach to the content?
Record Any Questions You Have Here

2

Align Content Standards to the Real World

> How can I co-create an authentic project challenge that aligns to my content standards?

We became educators because we have a passion for working with kids and by the fourth grade we have a preference for teaching a particular subject(s). For those of us who are at the middle school level, we more than likely received our certification in a content area because we enjoy that subject. Of course, there may be some courses we prefer over others and some units that excite us more than the rest. However, barring the occasional rough day, we love our profession and feel fortunate to help shape the lives of the older children and young teens entrusted to us to mentor and support. Consequently, we often believe our learners should share our passion for being in school and for learning the content we so enjoy teaching. The reality, of course, is that many of our learners go through the motions of school, while others may outright reject school.

Frequently, districts use project-based learning as a call to action to develop a more engaging pedagogical approach for their learners. Unfortunately, almost as often, PBL becomes the flavor of the day where by a three-day, "once and done" training takes place, and every teacher is expected to implement two projects before the end of the school year. Fast-forward a year or two on from the training and far fewer teachers continue to implement PBL. For some, the departure comes as a result of a refocusing of district efforts to the latest educational initiative, while others blame a lack of emphasis on the content and standards within the projects. You might even be reading this book as a victim of a similar scenario. To shift this narrative of a PBL story gone wrong, we must create an authentic challenge that meets our standards and also does so in a way that provides each learner with the appropriate level of support as they investigate the challenge. As such, you do not want to launch a challenge and expect your learners, on their own, to solve the challenge without any sort of facilitated guidance; believe me, you don't get to sit at your desk and drink coffee while your learners have at it! Instead, the revised Bloom's Taxonomy (Table 2.1) should be used as a lens for designing our authentic challenges, while our Stages of Project Assessment create a space to ensure the cultivation of our learners as agile and innovative problem-solvers.

Let's face it, you teach a class of learners who have varying levels of knowledge, experiences, skills, and aptitudes related to the standards our schools require us to teach. This can be both rewarding and frustrating at times. As a result, we must focus on differentiation within our lessons. However, traditional lesson planning often leaves little room for significant differentiation, or it requires a great deal of time and energy to find the appropriate resources and activities to support each individual learner or small groups of learners. As we shift to an authentic learning challenge, we now have greater flexibility for differentiation.

If we develop or co-design our challenge at the creation level of Bloom's, we provide the open-ended possibilities for inquiry and discovery that allow the appropriate level of complexity to emerge for each learner. Moreover, the creation level of Bloom's calls our learners to action as they consider a variety of solution outcomes. For our more advanced learners, we expect more complex thinking to reflect a deeper mastery of the standards. For our learners who struggle a bit more, we can tailor the learning experience to the appropriate level of complexity for them. Overall, the same challenge meets all of our learners where they are, as those that are gifted do not hit a ceiling in their learning and subsequently become bored, and those that need greater scaffolds and supports have the opportunity to rise to the challenge. Summarily, to provide a learning ecosystem that meets the needs of all of our learners, we must support them at each level of Bloom's.

We begin Stage One of our project at the creation level of Bloom's to launch our learners into the inquiry process that begins in this stage, and that then becomes the focus of Stage Two. Therefore, we embed our standards aligned to each level of Bloom's to scaffold and help our learners answer their inquiry question pathways that emanate from the challenge.

Furthermore, the use of Bloom's enables you to evaluate your learners as they move through each project assessment stage. Thus, we can appropriately differentiate our instruction where and when needed to ensure all of our learners complete the challenge at a level that exhibits their mastery of the standards for our classes.

How can I co-create an authentic project challenge that aligns to my content standards? Traditionally, many units start with a lesson that covers the basics of our content and then levels up to support our learners to attain mastery of the standards that frame it. We determine what lessons we need to build our learners up to the higher levels of thinking so that they are ready, by the end of the unit, to engage in critical thinking as they answer a document-based question on a test or perform a mathematical computation that is of increased complexity. However, once we reframe our approach to lesson planning in an authentic project context, the standards that we intend to meet through the project process are brought to life through the challenge rather than seen as a series of check-listed items for learners to master. Consequently, our learners see the relevance in the standards and are guided to meet higher levels of mastery of those standards with a targeted purpose behind their incorporation in the learning experience.

A higher level of standards mastery necessitates that our learners reach the creation level of Bloom's Taxonomy. To do so, we must write an open-ended, authentic challenge. This open-endedness allows for our pathways of inquiry as our learners uncover potential solutions that are appropriate for the context of the challenge and the intended end-user for the solution. As I noted in Chapter 1, we must be careful to ensure we don't push for our preconceived ideas about the desired outcome of a challenge. In fact, it is all too easy to write a faux challenge question that inserts your intended solution as part of the question. Take this example into consideration, "How can we make our roads safer by designing a new stop sign?" The question does not allow open-ended possibilities for a solution. Here, in this example, we have told our learners they will design a new stop sign and that the stop sign is what will make our roads safer. While this may seem like a silly example, it beautifully illustrates my point. The question provided them with the solution even though it didn't tell our learners how to design the new stop sign. Thus, we would want to rewrite the question as, "How can we make our roads safer?" Depending on your grade level or content area, the complexity of this question evolves. It is also important to note that we don't want to ask a question that is not aligned to our standards. While it may seem like a good community service opportunity, unless it directly aligns to your standards, it might be better suited for an afterschool club if you ask your learners, "How can we reduce the amount of litter in our school's neighborhood?"

In Table 2.1, take note of the developed questions, aligned to Bloom's, that you will use to assess your learners at each stage of the project. While these are intended as assessment guides, you may also use them to consider what lessons you might need to plan to support your learners at each stage and for each level of Bloom's. How will these lessons ensure you can adequately answer the listed questions as you formatively assess your learners? How does each lesson support your learners in their pursuit of devising an appropriate solution for the context of the project? As you consider these questions, please note that we write and introduce the project challenge at the creation level. However, creation is actually aligned to Stage Five when our learners have developed an actionable solution for their end-users. This alignment to Bloom's was an important part of the discovery and development process that Jill Ackers and I underwent during the writing of our PreK-3 book. It was our "ah ha" moment, if you will, and I hope it is an "ah ha" moment for you, as well.

I've already mentioned the importance of writing the authentic project challenge at the creation level of Bloom's. This open-ended opportunity for endless possible solutions allows for complexity to emerge for our learners.

Table 2.1 Project Assessment Stages Using Bloom's

Assessing Learners Through the Stages of a Project	Revised Bloom's Taxonomy	
Stage One: Challenge and Purpose How do we know if our learners understand and are invested in the challenge?	Understanding	Remembering is embedded within every complex layer of the project
Stage Two: Inquiry and Ideas How do we know if our learners have explored multiple pathways to a solution?	Applying	
Stage Three: Context and Perspective How do we know if our learners have considered end-user needs and technical expert feedback?	Analyzing	
Stage Four: Actions and Consequences How do we know if our learners have considered the potential positive and negative impacts of their proposed solution?	Evaluating	
Stage Five: Options and Opportunities How do we know if our learners have developed an actionable solution for their end-users?	Creating	

Writing these questions is an art; don't be discouraged if it takes you a while to master the process. I promise they will begin to come naturally after considerable practice. In the meantime, consider these four points to help you craft an authentic and relevant challenge question that will meet your learners at the appropriate levels of complexity (Laur & Ackers, 2017).

Crafting an Authentic and Relevant Challenge Question

1. **Start the question by making it personal.** "How can I ... ?" or "How can we ...?" are two of my favorite challenge starters. This question starter creates buy-in for our learners and provides a more relevant context.
2. **Make the question actionable.** At the heart of creation, our learners should produce something new or combine parts to make a whole for a new context. Design, develop, create, modify, produce, and plan are some of my favorite question starters, as these verbs reach the creation level of Bloom's.
3. **Don't create a question that merely asks for a yes or no answer.** This limited answer expectation is at a much lower level of Bloom's and subsequently limits the ability for our learners to engage in inquiry.
4. **Be sure that there isn't one right answer to your challenge.** If you anticipate receiving final products that will all look the same, go back and do some revision. While you want to meet your standards through the question, there is no standard final product in a genuinely authentic challenge.

Now, take the time to reflect on what you have learned in this chapter and on how to write open-ended challenges and the scaffolded questions that align with Bloom's. I have provided an earth science example regarding the study of soil erosion in Table 2.2 to help guide you. Keep in mind that my challenge question at the creation level of Bloom's, as it is listed here, went through several iterations before I settled on it. You, too, will probably find that your first attempts at writing challenge questions won't be perfect.

In Table 2.2, I have included the scaffolded Bloom's questions that help your learners through the inquiry process. I use these questions to help me determine what lessons I may need to develop as supports for my learners as they engage in inquiry. While I provided one question per level, you will want to incorporate as many appropriate questions that you need to meet your standards and the demands of your course. For practice, go back to

Table 2.2 Questions Through Bloom's

Creating	How can we effectively prevent soil erosion on our school grounds?
Evaluating	What are the most successful and cost-effective ways of controlling soil erosion?
Analyzing	How successful have soil erosion control plans been in a given topography compared to other areas?
Applying	What are ways we can mitigate soil erosion in different environments?
Understanding	What are the various classifications of soil?
Remembering	How do we identify soil erosion?

Table 1.3 in Chapter 1, and write a possible question for the listed challenges. I invite you to explore the suggested answers in Appendix 3 after you have tried to write your own. Table 2.4 is also an opportunity to enhance your challenge writing skills.

Real-world challenges connect our learners to the passions we have in the classroom and bring meaning to the required standards. However, we must be careful to ensure we don't let our enthusiasm for a challenge overlook what is relevant to our learners. Thus, we need to prepare to allow our learners to, in some instances, co-design the learning experience with us. As education experts in our curriculum, we should easily be able to connect any challenge that interests our learners to the standards we must teach. Thus, instead of approaching our lessons from a standards and content coverage viewpoint, we allow our learners to uncover the meaning of the standards through the inquiry process.

Additionally, we must ensure our standards ground our project work with a value-add to our curriculum. Otherwise, the project is merely an add-on that generally comes at the conclusion of our state testing or during the week before winter or spring break. Thus, choosing the aligned content, skills, and standards to weave throughout the project is a crucial first step in designing an effective, authentic learning experience.

As you explore the challenge ideas listed in Table 2.4, you will notice the link to national standards. Even if you teach a course that isn't tied to a set of national standards, more than likely, your curriculum has been written to reflect the national standards on some level. In Table 2.4, I list multiple standards from the Common Core in ELA and math, in addition to several Next Generation Science Standards. As a more targeted connection to authentic learning, the national standards for social studies, and the C3 Framework (College, Career, and Civic Readiness), list the following standards for learners to meet at the end of grade five and at the end of grade eight in Dimension 1: Constructing Compelling Questions:

- D1.1.3–5. Explain why compelling questions are important to others (e.g., peers, adults).
- D1.2.3–5. Identify disciplinary concepts and ideas associated with a compelling question that are open to different interpretations.
- D1.1.6–8. Explain how a question represents key ideas in the field.
- D1.2.6–8. Explain points of agreement experts have about interpretations and applications of disciplinary concepts and ideas associated with a compelling question.

Choose Appropriate Content and Skills

There is usually at least one unit that we can't wait to tackle and one that we may dread. If you dread a particular unit, please don't choose this one as your starting point. If you struggle to teach that unit traditionally, chances are you will struggle to turn it into an authentic challenge as well. I don't want you to get frustrated before you become more comfortable with designing authentic learning experiences. Therefore, it may be easier to start by picking a unit of study that you enjoy teaching. Whether it is a theme in world history dedicated to ancient civilizations or a focus on evolution in life science, you can probably think of numerous activities and lessons your learners enjoyed in the past. However, as you shift your focus to how to target an authentic and relevant approach to your content that supports the addressed standards, don't hold onto those past plans too tightly – I don't want your vision to be clouded too much. However, it is possible that you already have a semi-authentic project plan that only needs a few tweaks. In any case, open yourself to endless possibilities as you begin to plan, design, and create.

Many first-time PBL teachers prefer to start with the standards as the more comfortable approach to designing an authentic learning experience. Starting with your standards provides a guaranteed academic foundation for the project. From here, you can identify real-world connections that emerge from the standards. This approach to development and planning does mean that you are unlikely to co-design with your learners. However, not to worry as the more frequently you implement PBL, the more confident you will eventually become with the co-design ecosystem.

If you are a big idea person, it is highly likely that you feel comfortable enough to start with a project concept before moving on to the standards. Generally, the longer you have taught a subject, the more attuned you are to the standards and their connection to the world outside of the classroom. It isn't uncommon to hear a news story, read an article or book, or experience an event that gets your creative juices flowing. For example, every time I buy something from Amazon, I'm convinced there is a way to solve the following challenge: "How can we design a new system for shipping items from Amazon so that fewer or smaller boxes are used?" Similarly, sixth-grade math teacher, Holly Simmons at Elkin City Schools in Elkin, North Carolina, and I discussed this possibility in a coaching session, and Holly was immediately able to connect this project idea to her standards on volume and surface area.

Sometimes our standards are written as a checklist of what our learners should know by the end of the year. However, we can take this checklist and shift it to a world outside of the classroom approach. If you are currently looking at your standards and wondering how to do this, ponder the following social studies example. For this example, I will use the Virginia Standards of Learning (SOLs) as inspiration since Virginia is not a Common Core state. If you peruse the fourth-grade health SOLs, you will see a list of how learners must demonstrate, recognize, explain, and describe a variety of healthy decisions. Even if you aren't a health teacher, you can probably guess them: germs, physical activity, serving sizes, healthy foods, safety practices, and avoidance skills. These "standards" are more of a checklist, and if you were to use them as stand-alone mini-units on each subtopic, you would effectively never be able to get through your course with a PBL approach. Moreover, if you did, it is likely that you would have your learners complete a project rather than an authentic learning experience. Thus, in this case, I suggest you think more holistically and use a theme of standards to create the challenge. "How can we create a healthier population of students at our school?"

For this challenge, the theme of healthy decisions carries throughout each subtopic, and thus all of the required standards can be met in the process. As a requirement of the challenge, you could instruct your learners to use a minimum of two or three examples from each subtopic to support their solution. Your learners could then share their ideas with your administration and food service teams who have the power to enact any changes suggested by your learners. However, to level up the authenticity of our audience, the inclusion of technical experts such as an exercise physiologist or dietician is recommended.

This health example is dually inquiry-based, as well as standards-based. Sometimes, however, our standards may not overtly exhibit the real-world connections that we would like to make. Take a look at the following C3 Framework standards in Table 2.3 to illustrate this point.

Now, let's review an example of a relevant and authentic challenge linked to our learners' everyday lives with the standards listed in Table 2.3.

Table 2.3 C3 Framework Standards

D2.Civ.7.6–8.
Apply civic virtues and democratic principles in school and community settings.

D2.Civ.10.6–8.
Explain the relevance of personal interests and perspectives, civic virtues, and democratic principles when people address issues and problems in government and civil society.

D2.Civ.12.6–8.
Assess specific rules and laws (both actual and proposed) as means of addressing public problems.

D2.Eco.1.6–8.
Explain how economic decisions affect the well-being of individuals, businesses, and society.

D2.His.12.6–8.
Use questions generated about multiple historical sources to identify further areas of inquiry and additional sources.

D2.His.14.6–8.
Explain multiple causes and effects of events and developments in the past.

D2.Geo.2.6–8.
Use maps, satellite images, photographs, and other representations to explain relationships between the locations of places and regions, and changes in their environmental characteristics.

D2.Geo.4.6–8.
Explain how cultural patterns and economic decisions influence environments and the daily lives of people in both nearby and distant places.

Consider a traditional unit for a social studies class. No matter where we teach, how do these standards connect to our learners' everyday lives? From here, we look at the standards that relate to the content, as well as the lives of our learners.

You could begin the launch of the challenge by showing your learners a Google Earth view of your downtown community or taking a walking tour of the community. (If you don't have a downtown, that's okay, too.) Ideally, your town has either abandoned properties, as most do, or vacant areas ready for revitalization. The Google Earth or walking tour should spark a discussion between your learners about what your community has to offer, what it lacks, and what it needs. If your community already has a revitalization committee, now is an excellent time to partner with this organization and have them help launch the challenge: "How can we revitalize our downtown?"

I have worked with several schools that have implemented slight variations on this challenge from fourth to eighth grades. These schools have also added in math, ELA, and even science standards through an interdisciplinary approach to the challenge. In some cases, the partnership with the revitalization committee has led to more specific challenges dependent on the committee's needs and focus. This committee also serves as a feedback partner during Stage Three of the Project Assessment and as an authentic end-user audience for your learners during Stage Five.

Table 2.4 provides you with examples of challenges that address any number of subject areas and links them to national standards. I'm confident you will find your district standards easily align with these ideas. Notice how, in all of these examples, you could choose to create an interdisciplinary project with your colleagues or decide to implement the project within your course while exposing your learners to other subject areas within the context of the project (Laur & Ackers, 2017). Furthermore, almost every conceivable challenge has the potential to align to math and ELA standards through data analysis, reading, and writing. Please note, however, that the standards listed in Table 2.4 are not the full complement of what could evolve into the suggested challenges.

An interdisciplinary project obviously requires the inclusion of multiple standards. However, at the start of our PBL journey, we may or may not be ready to create an interdisciplinary project. If you are sticking with a project for your own content area, I cannot give you an exact number of standards to include in your project design. While some PBL experts advise that you only choose one or two "power" standards, I suggest you find the common threads throughout your curriculum and identify the standards that may fit together, even if they are designed for incorporation into separate chapters or units of study. Use their commonality to decide how and when these standards are used in the real world. By using only one or two standards, the depth of the challenge is limited, and the amount of time you devote to the work is too extensive. Additionally, with the use of only a few power standards, there is no possible way to effectively change your pedagogical approach to PBL.

When we choose multiple standards by which to support our project, we create a deeper project altogether. We want our learners to make sense of seemingly disconnected ideas. The use of multiple standards helps us to move from an environment in which we teach separate lessons to one that reframes our approach, focused on the authentic challenge. This helps our learners to string together ideas that may have previously seemed isolated and unrelated.

Therefore, it is time, at the middle school level, to quit focusing on our content areas as if they were stand-alone subjects. (At the later elementary years, it may be easier to find our connections with fewer class changes and fewer teachers per grade level.) All contents have the opportunity to incorporate reading, writing, and, in many cases, mathematical computation. If this scares you, that's okay. Take a deep breath and envision the

Table 2.4 Standards Aligned With Possible Authentic Challenges

Course(s)	Example Standard(s)	Possible Authentic Challenge
History, Civics, ELA, Math	8.SP.A.4. Investigate patterns of association in bivariate data. D2.Civ.10.6–8. Explain the relevance of personal interests and perspectives, civic virtues, and democratic principles when people address issues and problems in government and civil society.	Write a bill proposal on a topic relevant to your community that includes statistical data analysis and present the plan to your local congressman.
ELA, History	CCSS.ELA.W.4.1. Write opinion pieces on topics or texts, supporting a point of view with reasons and information. CCSS.ELA.RL.4.5. Explain major differences between poems, drama, and prose, and refer to the structural elements of poems and drama when writing or speaking about a text.	Submit an original poem or editorial to a local news or community publication linked to a studied topic in social studies.
Science, Math, ELA, Social Studies	5.MD.C.3. Recognize volume as an attribute of solid figures and understand concepts of volume measurement. D2.Eco.13.9–12. Explain why advancements in technology and investments in capital goods and human capital increase economic growth and standards of living.	Develop a plan to reduce food waste in the cafeteria, or extend the plan to the community and beyond.
Science, Engineering, ELA, Math, Economics	7.G.B.6. Solve real-life and mathematical problems involving angle measure, area, surface area, and volume. MS-LS2-5. Evaluate competing design solutions for maintaining biodiversity and ecosystem services.	Develop an idea to eliminate the use of plastic in the school, the community, and beyond, or develop a replacement for a plastic item.
Economics, Social Studies	D2.Eco.7.6–8. Analyze the role of innovation and entrepreneurship in a market economy. D2.Eco.1.6–8. Explain how economic decisions affect the well-being of individuals, businesses, and society.	Develop a student-run business for the school with a required business plan to be presented to district administration for approval. Small business owners from the community provide feedback through the development process.

unlimited possibilities that can arise when we make the concerted effort to integrate our content areas. You may decide to start small as you bring the other content areas into your solo attempt at implementing a challenge, or you can go much bigger and forge a partnership with another teacher or teachers. Additionally, reading, writing, speaking, and listening standards are easily embedded into any content area that you teach. As our learners engage in a challenge, they require many opportunities to demonstrate their understanding of the standards, and you have an unlimited potential to embed standards from across disciplines to make the required learning become relevant. As these two ideas meet, from an assessment viewpoint, we see an increase in the mastery of the standards.

Using the given project idea in Table 2.4, reflect on the process of how to align your standards to an authentic challenge. Think about how the challenge and your learners' final product will meet the following goals.

Meeting Three Key Goals

1. **Space for innovation:**
   Our authentic challenges must have the potential for multiple interpretations of final products/solutions. As we write an open-ended challenge, we automatically create those multiple pathways for inquiry. These numerous pathways ensure all the products/solutions won't look similar. In fact, some of the authentic challenges that I implemented for several years never had the same result with each new crop of learners.

   Since I am sure you are wondering, if you haven't already inferred from my previous example statement, yes you can use the same project multiple times if, in fact, you make sure it allows for innovation. However, this scenario is very different from the coffee can totem pole project that my daughter had to craft in middle school to represent the spirit animals of our family. (I have kept those coffee cans in my basement for four years just so I could recycle that project!) Instead, think about it this way: your smartphone is on generation ten plus right now. The challenge that these companies face on a yearly or bi-yearly basis is, "How can we improve our smartphone features to meet the demands of our customers?" As a result, over the years, we have seen our phones change in size, battery capability, photo quality, fingerprint and face recognition, and a multitude of other features that are too numerous to mention. Thus, we can envision how an authentic challenge leaves plenty of space for innovation, even if we repurpose it.

2. **End-user connection:**
   In my first book, *Authentic Learning Experiences: A Real-World Approach to Project-Based Learning,* Chapter 3 discussed, in detail, the need to create a challenge that relates to either a community or career connection. While a career connection is mostly self-explanatory, be sure to move beyond a report of "this is what I need to know to work in this profession." On the other hand, a community connection is a bit more open to interpretation as it includes your school, local, state, national, or global community. However, as noted in goal number one, above, we must ensure our learners see the relevance in this community. Thus, using the health example from earlier in the chapter, our learners probably would not see the relevance of crafting a plan if they were not introduced to the idea that their presentation audience would include an exercise physiologist or dietician.

   Moreover, these products cannot simply live in a showcased experience that involves other students and parents. Instead, we need to ensure our learners share these products with an authentic audience who has the potential to effect the change our learners desire. For example, I once had a group of fifth-graders present their solutions to a group of second-graders. After the presentation, the fifth-graders declared it was a waste of their time since the second-grade class couldn't make their ideas happen, and they were right!

3. **Technical experts:**
   We may be the educational experts in the classroom, but we can't be expected to be an expert on all topics (Laur & Ackers, 2017). Unless we've had a job outside of education in a field that aligns to the content we teach, we are not technical experts in our subject area. (Keep in mind that technical does not mean technology!) For example, if you teach a computer coding class and were never a coder, you probably know more than enough qualifying information to teach the course, but you probably aren't able to design a code from scratch (not using Scratch) for an app that you would like to sell. Therefore, we fundamentally lack the technical expertise that can enrich our learners' experiences in an authentic challenge to a higher level. The value-added feedback that a technical expert can provide in an authentic challenge propels our learners into thinking about new perspectives and helps them to visualize the needs of their end-user to a higher degree. Thus, when we utilize technical experts, in person and virtually, we create multiple advantages for our learners to understand the context of the challenge from a more authentic perspective. Additionally, these experts may also be recruited

as our authentic audience in Stage Five and assist with the end-user connection that we seek to attain.

As seen in the example in Table 2.5, we included standards that come from the multiple disciplines of science, math, literacy, and writing. Therefore, the interdisciplinary connections between standards that lead to a challenge supported by multiple teachers are a better mirror the real world outside of the classroom. Once you become more attuned to the process of developing authentic challenges, the more opportunities you have to develop interdisciplinary problems, and the more your learners will see the value and importance in the standards.

Some content areas naturally align such as social studies and ELA. Science and math are frequently compatible partners, as much of the scientific process is deeply embedded in math (Laur & Ackers, 2017). However, data analysis in social studies is a great place to make a math connection as well. Cross-curricular ideas are also the perfect time to enlist the help of our elective teachers. We can also easily integrate art, music, and even physical education into an authentic project. For example, our health example from the Virginia Standards of Learning that we discussed earlier in the chapter focused on the question: "How can we create a healthier population of students at our school?" While the connection to health standards is readily apparent, and there is an easy link to a physical education component, we can also target math standards. While these subject areas are not normally considered planning partners, any data that our learners collect provides them with the occasion to visually represent it using any number of graphing options.

We have already reviewed how to start with a project idea and match it to our standards. Alternatively, we may be inspired by our learners' questions and ideas from which we then develop a challenge. This latter approach can be a bit tricky if you are bound by a scope and sequence to your curriculum. For those of you who are not, you may need to shift your schedule to incorporate a particular unit or content focus earlier or later in your school year.

Contemplate the following example: You have a group of learners walk into your morning class discussing the events of the previous day's news announcement that poverty and civic unrest are at an all-time high in your community. While, at first glance, this is a social studies concept and you teach ELA, you are excited at the prospect of tapping into the discussion. As an ELA teacher, you are aware that Lowry's *The Giver* is a recommended reading for your learners, and while this dystopian novel is focused on how the government can, on a grand scale, control how people act, the parallels are there. Instead of diving into your next grammar lesson, you decided to introduce the book this week. You quickly think on your feet, knowing full well you will have time to plan in

Table 2.5 Authentic Life Science Challenge Using Science, Math, and Literacy

Consider the following project idea:

You are concerned with the recent discovery of an area on your school campus near a stream that has slowly eroded after years of kids running up and down the incline coupled with a few severe rainy seasons. Currently, the district has done little to address the issue besides sending out an email asking teachers to do their best to prevent kids from accessing the area. Recently, one student fell down the muddy hill and, as a result, caused quite a commotion in the school. You know it is unlikely that any land remediation action will occur soon, and this issue relates to your upcoming unit on weathering and erosion.

You know that you want to include informational texts, mathematical modeling, and the Next Generation Science Standards that relate to Earth's surface (See the full version of the standards below.)*

You brainstorm possible events, people, and places that would allow your learners to demonstrate their understanding of soil erosion. You highlight these verbs as connectors to the summative assessment: **construct, write, develop, reason, solve**, and **assess**. You have decided not to include the verbs **gather, quote, use**, and **cite**, as these will support your big idea but don't go deep enough into Bloom's as part of the inquiry process. Next, you focus on how to write the challenge for your project. For this, you refer back to your revised Bloom's list of verbs and concentrate on the creation level. You ponder the question, "What could my learners develop that highlights their understanding of soil erosion and potentially effects change in their world?" After a period of contemplation, you settle on the following challenge:

"How can we effectively prevent soil erosion on our school grounds?"

Standards to Explore:

Next Generation Science Standards Addressed:

MS-ESS2.1–1. Develop a model to describe the cycling of Earth's materials and the flow of energy that drives this process.

MS-ESS2-2. Construct an explanation based on evidence for how geoscience processes have changed Earth's surface at varying time and spatial scales.

MS-ESS3-1. Construct a scientific explanation based on evidence for how the uneven distribution of Earth's mineral, energy, and groundwater resources are the result of past and current geoscience processes. [Clarification statement includes soil with locations of active weathering and/or disposition of rock.]

MS-LS2-5. Evaluate competing design solutions for maintaining biodiversity and ecosystem services.

CCSS ELA/Literacy Standards Addressed:

RST.6–8.1. Cite specific textual evidence to support analysis of science and technical texts.

RST.6–8.7. Integrate quantitative or technical information expressed in words in a text with a version of that information expressed visually.

WHST.6–8.2. Write informative/explanatory texts to examine a topic and convey ideas, concepts, and information through the selection, organization, and analysis of relevant content.

WHST.6–8.8. Gather relevant information from multiple print and digital sources, using search terms to effectively; assess the credibility and accuracy of each source; and quote or paraphrase the data and conclusions of others while avoiding plagiarism and following a standard format for citation.

SL.8.5. Integrate multimedia and visual displays into presentations to clarify information, strengthen claims and evidence, and add interest.

(Continued)

Table 2.5 (Cont).

CCSS Mathematics Standards Addressed:

MP.2. Reason abstractly and quantitatively.

7.EE.B.4. Use variables to represent quantities in a real-world or mathematical problem, and construct simple equations and inequalities to solve problems by reasoning about the quantities.

7.G.B.4. Solve real-life and mathematical problems involving angle measure, area, surface area, and volume.

Authentic Challenge Presented to Our Learners:

During the week, you take your class to visit the erosion site in question to allow your learners to make observations and inferences about the quality of the soil integrity. As you introduce the challenge, you present the following information:

Our soil is a complex, yet fragile, ecosystem made up of many living organisms and decomposing organic materials. The erosion of our soil leads to economic and environmental destruction. Your goal is to develop a plan to manage, and hopefully reverse, its damaging impact. Our presented project will be in front of the district grounds maintenance director, as well as a variety of other technical experts in the field. These experts will include representatives from the local conservation district and the Department of Environmental Protection for our state. Additionally, these technical experts will be on hand to provide you with feedback during the design process. You are expected to incorporate this feedback for your final proposal in your panel presentation, as well as include it in the more detailed, written proposal you submit to the panel.

---

more detail later. You start a discussion related to the news release, and to your delight the entire class begins debating the issue. In fact, one learner asks the question, "How can we improve our community to meet the needs of all of our citizens?" You decide to run with this challenge question and prepare to introduce *The Giver* as a case study for your learners to analyze as they investigate the question in more detail. Your mind is full of ideas and possibilities, but you also know your learners are ready to help you lead this charge and co-develop the learning experience with you. From this example, we can envision how amazing authentic challenges can emerge when we open ourselves to the possibilities that may exist within the inquiring minds of our learners. It is up to us to then make the connection to our standards.

Questions to Ask When Aligning Your Standards to a Project Challenge

I'm sure you have spent the whole of this chapter, as well as Chapter 1, thinking about possible ideas for an authentic challenge. I shared some ideas in Tables 1.4 and 2.4. At this point, it is a good idea to ask, "How can I maximize both my community assets and authentic challenges my community faces, to bring relevance to my standards and content?" This four-step question process will allow you to be successful in designing authentic challenges aligned to your standards (Laur & Ackers, 2017).

> **Step 1: To what challenges in my community will my learners make connections and provide possible solutions?**

As I mentioned in Chapter 1, some consider contrived scenarios as authentic PBL. While these are typical in many classrooms, I prefer to use them as a scaffold for a deeper authentic experience. Often, these scenario-based simulations stop at the applying level of Bloom's. True authentic learning experiences, for which there is no one right solution, automatically requires higher-order thinking. As our learners move beyond memorization of vocabulary words, formulas, facts, and dates, we can replace these frequently disassociated ideas that pervade some of the units we teach with a cohesively linked set of relevant experiences that are grounded in the real world.

Furthermore, true authentic projects move our learners beyond just writing about what they research. For example, in a cross-curricular approach to science and ELA, when given an assignment about diseases and disabilities, a teacher may instruct his learners to research the major illnesses and disabilities and their causes and effects. He may ask them to write a fictional story about a young child with a disability or terminal illness. The assignment could extend to writing an opinion paragraph about how the medical community should handle genetic testing and the ethics behind it. Additionally, to incorporate math standards, learners could analyze the current statistical data from the U.S. Centers of Disease Control or American Association of People with Disabilities and compare that analysis to the numbers from the last three decades. This example, however, does not push our learners into the highest levels of Bloom's. We have merely asked for existing research and an analysis of that research. There is no real relevance for completing the activity. Therefore, to make this activity an authentic challenge, we need an authentic community connection.

Instead, let's review the *Understanding Differences* project developed by a fifth-grade teacher, Jamie Hammond, of Dallastown, Pennsylvania, who invited her learners to participate in the challenge, "How can we create a product to help someone with a disability, disease, or disorder?" To introduce the challenge, Ms. Hammond shared a Fixperts video to pique her learners' interest in the topic. As the first few days of the challenge progressed, Ms. Hammond asked her learners to connect to someone in their lives who lives with a disease, disability, or disorder. Immediately, this connection brought relevance to the project as her learners had an opportunity to impact the life of someone for whom they cared. While some learners chose a family friend or relative, others decided to partner with a peer from their school. Throughout this project, her learners used the novel, *Out of My Mind*, as a case study for character analysis and evaluation of the plot, rising action, climax, falling action, and resolution. As her learners worked on developing their products, they connected with the STEAM lab teacher from the district, as well as a local occupational therapist, for feedback on their designs. At the conclusion of this project, Ms. Hammond's learners automatically had an authentic audience in their chosen end-users of their designed product. Moreover, the class submitted their ideas via videos to the Fixperts. In this contrasting example, Ms. Hammond created a relevant context for her literature content, as well as shifting the focus from elementary analysis and evaluation through discussions and writing to moving her learners into action.

> **Step 2: What technical experts are available for consultation in the design process and during the implementation of the project?**

If we struggle with how to develop an authentic challenge out of our given standards, now is the time to turn to a technical expert for advice. These technical experts live our content as part of their jobs, and they have varied experiences in their application. In some instances, our technical experts may even have an authentic project they would like your learners to assist them in completing! The use of these experts models your desire for lifelong learning and adds value to how your learners view you as someone ready to learn with them, rather than someone who merely tells them what to learn.

We can also use these technical experts to provide feedback to our learners during the project process. This feedback is most notably important during Stage Three as our technical experts provide our learners with a different perspective than they may have previously considered. Furthermore, our technical experts can ask profound questions about the proposed solutions in relation to their functional ability for their end-user audience. These technical experts can then become part of our authentic audience in Step Five of this process.

In the soil erosion example from earlier in this chapter, our teacher was not a soil scientist. While she certainly understood the standards and the basic ideas behind soil erosion, she still was not a technical expert as a soil scientist, environmental scientist, or conservation specialist. However, just as the technical experts were able to provide content-specific application in the design process, their feedback for the learners was equally invaluable. It helped our learners to modify and refine their ideas until they had perfected their designs to achieve the purpose of the challenge based on its specific context.

> **Step 3: How can products be learner-generated and aligned with my content and standards?**

While the product is the summative assessment we grade, the more critical aspect is how the end-user or authentic audience reacts to the final product/solution. Therefore, as we design our authentic project-based learning experience, it is sometimes necessary to have an idea in mind for a final product that is suitable for the audience. This final product could be a written or oral proposal, or it might take the format of any of the listed ideas in Table 1.4. However, we also know, that by this age, our learners are also capable of determining their final products. Moreover, it is entirely possible that your user-audience dictates the development of that final product. For example, if our learners are applying for a grant, they may be required to present at a community meeting, as well as submit the completed application of questions, charts, graphs, and budget allocations.

It isn't necessary to always require replication by every learner of the same summative product format. Depending on the project, you can let your learners decide for whom they design the final product and the final product form. You will, however, need to provide the criteria for the product to ensure you can equally assess each learner in the process. This criterion adds an authentic element to the challenge, as the world outside of the classroom operates under this same premise. Just as you are required to have a lesson plan with specific elements or a doctor must maintain a record of treatment for each patient, requirements are a part of real-life. Our project experiences should be no different. However, a genuinely open-ended challenge leaves lots of room for interpretation on how to answer it. As in our soil project example, we know our learners need to develop a solution to mitigate the effects of soil erosion on the school campus. However, we have no idea what solution they may develop or what inquiry pathway they may take to arrive at this solution. Thus, with a provision of requirements, we provide structure for the challenge, but, at the same time, we do not give a detailed plan for how our learners will achieve their goal.

> **Step 4: How can I incorporate technical experts as part of an authentic audience?**

For a project-based experience to be entirely authentic, it is vital that our learners share their solutions in some way with a public audience that consists of stakeholders in the challenge. All too frequently, we either skip this step due to a perceived lack of time, or we present to parents or other classes as an easy option. However, we must seek out technical experts who can genuinely offer a value-added opinion regarding the authentic challenge. This value-added feedback provides validation to the complex work our learners have engaged in during the learning experience.

As you choose your authentic audience, consider their ability to make your learners' solution to the challenge become a reality. We want our audience to have the power to potentially effect the change that has been requested by our learners. Whether or not this requested change becomes a reality is a moot issue, as we know, in real life, not every change we fight for happens. Thus, it is a good lesson in either case. An engaged stakeholder audience provides feedback for the acceptance or rejection of a proposed solution. And, even if a rejected solution results, learners have much to celebrate. The mere act of sharing one's mastery of the content and standards to an authentic audience means much more than any returned test graded by a teacher, no matter what grade is received.

Consider this example as a relevant connection to your learners' own challenges. Suppose your school has a problem with feral cats running about the property. Several learners are allergic to cats, and more annoyingly, the scat left behind by the cats has caused a problem for staff, parents, kids, and maintenance. This authentic challenge is the perfect opportunity for your learners to design a solution to the problem and present their findings to the school administration, district maintenance directors, and representative from animal control. The presence of this authentic audience automatically makes your learners' products real for a challenge that is relevant to them.

While I encourage a live audience for a panel presentation whenever possible and appropriate, you do not need to have a formal presentation of learning (POL) that looks much like a science fair exhibit. Many PBL schools use this format, and I am not a fan of it. These POLs might invite experts to roam around the exhibits and make general comments. Typically, parents and the community are invited as a poor substitute for the real technical experts.

There are other options for sharing your learners' work with an authentic audience that doesn't require the time or the effort to secure a panel of technical experts such as those listed in our feral cat example. In some instances, it may be more appropriate for your learners to send off their final products for review digitally. An electronic submission or an actual product delivered to a location is perfectly acceptable as an alternative to an onsite presentation. In either case, the audience must still be authentic for the challenge to be meaningful. For example, in Jamie's Understanding Differences project, it wasn't feasible to invite the Fixperts organization into her classroom. The main Fixperts group is located in London, England! In each instance, onsite or virtually, the audience is equally authentic. What we don't want to happen is to have our learners randomly post their work online in the hopes that someone may stumble across it.

When it is a viable option, public presentations help our learners to develop and refine their communication skills, as they become more comfortable in front of adult audiences. Speaking in front of an adult audience of technical experts creates a sense of empowerment when change is effected as a result of their ideas. To enhance this step, a move to a venue outside of the classroom makes the experience even more authentic, as the walls of the classroom are literally removed. An example of this offsite presentation includes meeting with that technical expert in his or her office.

Not only does moving a presentation outside of the school walls provide a more authentic context to the project, it also increases the connection our learners have to their community. One such example includes a local theater that might be interested in showcasing student-created dramas regarding how to address bullying issues. Similarly, merely taking our learners onsite to the location in question makes the presentation more authentic for our audience. For instance, a trip to the local zoning board for the township in which the learners present to the board of commissioners regarding their ideas on how to revitalize the downtown area provides added value to the meaning behind the presentation as it requires a more professional approach, rather than simply inviting the commissioners into our classroom space.

If the consideration of moving your learners to an offsite location seems like a daunting task due to your rural area or the cost of hiring a school bus for a field trip, think about virtual opportunities. Online organizations such as Nepris work tirelessly to connect classrooms to experts. Real World Scholars is another online asset that provides web hosting space for classes and, as a side benefit, provides Nepris at no cost to their classes. If you are up for the challenge, reach out to experts via LinkedIn or Twitter. You never know who might respond! A Zoom session with the technical experts you find or a videotaped presentation to send to your audience is an effective alternative to an onsite presentation. In any case, the culmination of your challenge as it is shared, in some way, with an authentic audience creates significant meaning of the unit content and promotes the ultimate mastery of the standards.

It is entirely possible for our learners to be both engaged and empowered in our classrooms, while simultaneously mastering our standards. Rote memorization of content and the application of our standards in a mid-level push for Bloom's are easily a thing of the past, as we move into much deeper authentic learning experiences. Here, both the complexity and the relevance of our classroom ecosystem push our standards to an authentic level that helps to write the educational story we want our learners to write and remember.

Time to Reflect

1. What standards that you teach connect directly to the possible community resources and technical experts from Chapter 1?

2. In what ways are the standards you are considering linked to a possible real-world challenge?

3. What authentic end products might best demonstrate your learners' understanding of the content and the standards for a possible authentic challenge?

Record Any Questions You Have Here

3

Support Digital Transformation

> How can I embed instructional technology into my authentic challenge to transform the learning experience in my classroom?

Just over a decade ago, I was fortunate enough to be a part of a grant program supported by the Commonwealth of Pennsylvania. The grant program was entitled Classrooms for the Future, and I received a classroom set of laptops with an interactive whiteboard. To be eligible for the program, I was required to take a few graduate courses that I crazily started two weeks after my second child was born. These classes changed my perspective on project-based learning entirely. While these few required courses eventually turned into a second master's degree in 21st Century Teaching and Learning, initially, I had the opportunity to investigate PBL, authentic learning, and inquiry-based learning. It was then that I realized these core pedagogical approaches are fundamentally linked with the same underpinning: asking questions to uncover solutions to challenges.

A lot of my educational beliefs of today have been shaped from the time I spent as a Classrooms for the Future teacher. Moreover, I was also fortunate to teach in a district that was forward-thinking, supportive of any new ideas I wanted to try, and provided me with a fantastic instructional technology coach, Sue Sheffer. While she probably doesn't remember many of the conversations we had or the times she spent working with me,

I will never forget the impact of her standard question: "Why do you want to use that new tool?"

It was probably mid-2008 or early 2009, and I had just returned from some professional development session that showcased the use of Wikispaces (may it rest in peace) in the classroom. I was excited and ready to jump into planning my next project idea centered on using a wiki. I distinctly recall sitting in our tiny, windowless planning room, chattering about how wikis were going to change my life when Sue stopped me cold.

> *Sue:* Why do you want to use a wiki?
> *Me:* Well, the lady leading the training showed us, and it looked pretty awesome.
> *Sue:* I'm sure it did. But, why do you really want to use a wiki?
> *Me:* I want my students to journal as a reflection tool during their project.
> *Sue:* What's the purpose of a wiki?
> *Me:* I'm pretty sure it is a collaborative tool that students can use to build pages of content.
> *Sue:* Then is a wiki your best option for what you want to do?
> *Me:* Can't I make it work for what I want it to do?
> *Sue:* I think we should talk about starting a blog.

While the conversation reflects the era of Web 2.0 tools that were all the rage in the latter half of the first decade of this century, it also reflects the essential need to stop and consider why we might use one digital tool over another or why we want to use technology applications in the first place. Keep in mind that it isn't necessary to incorporate any form of digital technology into your authentic challenges. So, if you are in a position of limited access to computers or the Internet, you can make adjustments as needed. If you are in a situation of limited access, perhaps you want to have your learners explore the very authentic and relevant challenge: "How can we increase our access to technology tools at school?"

"Instructional technology" is a phrase we must define before we move forward in answering our challenge question for this chapter. Instruction, of course, is merely something that is intended for use in teaching. I know there are many instructional techniques and pedagogies out there. In case you haven't figured it out, I'm impartial to the use of an authentic project-based approach to instruction. The definition of technology, however, may get a bit fuzzy. Please don't confuse technology with digital tools. While digital tools can indeed be used to support technology, technically they are not technology per se. Instead, let's think about technology as the application of knowledge in a particular area.

SAMR and ISTE

One popular standard of thinking about the integration of digital tools into the classroom is the SAMR model. Designed by Dr. Ruben Puentedura in the early part of the 21st century, SAMR categorizes the levels in which we implement digital tools into lessons and pedagogical approaches across all grade levels and content areas (Hamilton, Rosenberg, & Akcaoglu, 2016). SAMR (substitution, augmentation, modification, and realization) aligns to our model of authentic learning and, in effect, mirrors much of what we have discussed regarding Bloom's.

From the substitution level, the tools we use have no effective change in our classroom practice. Instead of writing notes on the board for our learners to copy, we may simply put the notes in a PowerPoint presentation with fancy graphics and flashy transitions. At the end of the class period, however, the outcome is the same in both cases; our learners have merely copied notes. Of course, our goal is not only to change the implementation of digital technology tools at the substitution level but also to shift how our learners consume any information in our classes. While an occasional mini-lecture may serve an appropriate purpose, our learners should be gathering data and research during the inquiry phase of Stage Two. The substitution level of projects is having our learners complete a guided task, step-by-step, instead of a test. While you may consider ditching your tests in favor of a project-based learning experience, this step-by-step model is not an element of an authentic challenge.

In the augmentation level of SAMR, we use the tool for substitution purposes, but we do see a useful change in how we use it. An example of augmentation is the use of any online quizzing system that provides immediate feedback to our learners regarding correct and incorrect answers. In the context of a project, it is helpful to utilize online databases and tools such as NetTrekker and Diigo that I discuss in Chapter 4.

SAMR's modification tier provides the opportunity for extensive changes in how a learner completes a task through the use of digital tools. While most of these activities will fall in the analysis and evaluation levels of Bloom's, modification still falls short on our authentic learning scale. An example of how a project meets modification is when we ask our learners to create a video book trailer of a novel instead of a traditional book report. Many teachers mistakenly consider modification as the creation level of Bloom's.

The argument generally unfolds that the "creation" of a book trailer, or any other creation of an artifact for that matter, is at the highest level of Bloom's. However, we must go back to my research paper in disguise comment from Chapter 1. While the artifact is a creation, it is not the creation of new information; it is merely a modification of information that they could otherwise share in a more traditional manner.

Finally, the pinnacle of SAMR, redefinition, presents our learners with a digital environment to complete a task that previously could not have occurred. An example of how redefinition impacts an authentic learning experience relates to Stage Three when our learners can connect with technical experts for feedback in an online environment. This connection is especially important for our rural areas where access was previously limited. Additionally, if you think about an authentic challenge as a whole, we are asking our learners to redefine how they learn and approach a problem. Instead of providing our learners with the desired answer through resources and information, we reverse that mentality and ask our learners to redefine the problem through an actionable solution that has the potential to effect change.

As we enter into the third decade of the 21st century, more than ten years after SAMR was first introduced, the way in which we use technology tools in the classroom has shifted. However, I am not convinced it has shifted rapidly enough to mirror the technological changes outside of the classroom. To illustrate this evolution, let's review the *International Society for Technology Education* (ISTE) standards for students and their transformation over the last two decades (see Table 3.1).

When I first reviewed the overarching categories for the ISTE Standards for Students in 2016, I was impressed at the lack of reference to technology from an education technology association. Unlike the standards discussed in Chapter 2, these standards are not linked to testing or specific content. However, the context in which you apply them aligns to the design of authentic learning experiences. Likewise, the standards line up with our project assessment stages to illustrate the connection between the transformation of our learners and the skills, knowledge, and attributes they gain through the project process.

Table 3.1 ISTE Standards Transformation

Year	ISTE Standards Focus
1998	Student productivity through the use of technology tools (i.e. spreadsheets and word processing) in a computer lab
2007	Teach essential skills (i.e. communication, collaboration, critical thinking) through the use of technology via mobile carts
2016	Transforming learning beyond the classroom made possible through handheld technology

The seven, over-arching categories from which the ISTE standards emanate and to which we align our project assessment stages are listed in Table 3.2.

Each of these seven standards contains four additional sub-standards that further explain the goal to which our learners should strive in the classroom. It is up to us, as facilitators of the learning process, to ensure they reach the pinnacle of these standards. While there is no exact rubric aligned to the basic, proficient, or advanced categories our learners might achieve for these standards, we can cite specific evidence of how an authentic challenge incorporates each of these standards. Additionally, our questions that align with the Five Stages of Project Assessment exemplify how we can assess the mastery of these standards (Table 3.3).

As you review each of these ISTE standards, consider the impact of your design and assessment of your authentic challenge and how they both elevate your learners to meet each of the ISTE standard themes. In other words, think about how your challenge makes your learners empowered through the process of solving the problem, as they construct knowledge rather than merely consume information. Furthermore, contemplate how your learners have the opportunity to engage in computational thinking as they innovate designs of new solutions. All the while, your learners should enhance their abilities to creatively

Table 3.2 ISTE Standards for Students

ISTE Standard Theme	Standard Explanation
Empowered Learner (1)	Students leverage technology to take an active role in choosing, achieving and demonstrating competency in their learning goals, informed by the learning sciences.
Digital Citizen (2)	Students recognize the rights, responsibilities and opportunities of living, learning and working in an interconnected digital world, and they act and model in ways that are safe, legal and ethical.
Knowledge Constructor (3)	Students critically curate a variety of resources using digital tools to construct knowledge, produce creative artifacts and make meaningful learning experiences for themselves and others.
Innovative Designer (4)	Students use a variety of technologies within a design process to identify and solve problems by creating new, useful or imaginative solutions.
Computational Thinker (5)	Students develop and employ strategies for understanding and solving problems in ways that leverage the power of technological methods to develop and test solutions.
Creative Communicator (6)	Students communicate clearly and express themselves creatively for a variety of purposes using the platforms, tools, styles, formats and digital media appropriate to their goals.
Global Collaborator (7)	Students use digital tools to broaden their perspectives and enrich their learning by collaborating with others and working effectively in teams locally and globally.

Table 3.3 Assessment Stages Aligned to ISTE Standards

Project Assessment Stages	ISTE Standards for Students
Stage One: Challenge and Purpose How do we know if our learners understand and are invested in the challenge?	3d – Students build knowledge by actively exploring real-world issues and problems, developing ideas and theories and pursuing answers and solutions. 4a – Students know and use a deliberate design process for generating ideas, testing theories, creating innovative artifacts or solving authentic problems. 7d – Students explore local and global issues and use collaborative technologies to work with others to investigate solutions.
Stage Two: Inquiry and Ideas How do we know if our learners have explored multiple pathways to a solution?	3a – Students plan and employ effective research strategies to locate information and other resources for their intellectual or creative pursuits. 4c – Students develop, test and refine prototypes as part of a cyclical design process. 5b – Students collect data or identify relevant data sets, use digital tools to analyze them, and represent data in various ways to facilitate problem-solving and decision-making.
Stage Three: Context and Perspective How do we know if our learners have considered end-user needs and technical expert feedback?	1c – Students use technology to seek feedback that informs and improves their practice and to demonstrate their learning in a variety of ways. 7a – Students use digital tools to connect with learners from a variety of backgrounds and cultures, engaging with them in ways that broaden mutual understanding and learning. 7b – Students use collaborative technologies to work with others, including peers, experts or community members, to examine issues and problems from multiple viewpoints.
Stage Four: Actions and Consequences How do we know if our learners have considered the potential positive and negative impacts of their proposed solution?	2c – Students demonstrate an understanding of and respect for the rights and obligations of using and sharing intellectual property. 5c – Students break problems into component parts, extract key information, and develop descriptive models to understand complex systems or facilitate problem-solving. 6a – Students choose the appropriate platforms and tools for meeting the desired objectives of their creation or communication.
Stage Five: Options and Opportunities How do we know if our learners have developed an actionable solution for their end-users?	3c – Students curate information from digital resources using a variety of tools and methods to create collections of artifacts that demonstrate meaningful connections or conclusions.

(Continued)

Table 3.3 (Cont).

Project Assessment Stages	ISTE Standards for Students
	4d – Students exhibit a tolerance for ambiguity, perseverance, and the capacity to work with open-ended problems.
	6d – Students publish or present content that customizes the message and medium for their intended audiences.

communicate as they globally collaborate, and do so in such a way that supports their digital citizenship. Let's explore Table 3.2 in more detail in the sections below.

> **Stage One: Challenge and Purpose**
>
> How do we know if our learners understand and are invested in the challenge?

While the purpose of the challenge for our learners may vary from challenge to challenge, our aim in designing and assessing a problem stems from the desire to ensure our learners become knowledge constructors who go beyond low-level Bloom's thinking. I have discussed quite a bit about Bloom's in Chapters 1 and 2, and I would be remiss if I didn't revisit it here. We want our learners to craft solutions that are novel in their application to the given problem. As such, the creation level of Bloom's aligns to our learners as knowledge constructors.

Since we want to start an authentic project before we have taught any of the content, this leaves the door open to allow our learners to become knowledge constructors. As they explore the authentic issue, they begin to develop potential pathways for exploration, and possible solutions to the challenge begin to materialize. Constructing knowledge automatically leaves the door open for the emergence of innovative designs. Here, as our learners start to define their purpose for the learning experience, they also begin to generate ideas they want to explore in more detail and theories they will have to test to settle on an inquiry path of choice.

As we began to think about our authentic challenge design in Chapters 1 and 2, the need for a connection to an issue that was not only real world but also meaningful to our learners became evident. Thus, local connections are often our starting point for design. However, resident issues are not the only option for exploration. Global problems have the power of relevancy for our learners when they can empathize and understand how these issues have either direct or indirect ties to their lives. Often, local issues have a global context for comparison, as well. Therefore, the use of collaborative technologies to connect our learners with the world beyond the classroom presents as a deeper purpose for the challenge. Explore the digital tools in Table 3.4 to envision how you might enhance the learning experience in Stage One.

> **Stage Two: Inquiry and Ideas**
>
> How do we know if our learners have explored multiple pathways to a solution?

As our learners delve into the inquiry process, we must be sure they are prepared to plan and carry out research strategies that effectively assist them in locating the appropriate resources to help them solve the presented challenge. Of course, it is perfectly acceptable to assist in this process as we gather and make available a variety of primary and secondary sources for review. This predetermined list of sources ensures we facilitate the journeys our learners take down their chosen inquiry pathway without directing the trip. Indeed, our learners will also contribute resources. However, depending on their grade level, reading level, and skill level, these resources may only be a supplement to our already provided sources.

In addition to provided and independently discovered primary and secondary sources, I suggest you facilitate opportunities for your learners to connect with what their end-users want in a solution. To fully engage in the inquiry process such that our learners begin to consider their end-users, it is imperative that our learners consider how they can collect additional data to justify their ideas. This data, when visually represented, then serves as a way to persuade their authentic audience that their generated ideas are, in fact, viable solutions to the challenge they should consider.

Our learners may generate initial ideas in Stage One before they jump heavily into the inquiry practice of Stage Two. Once they have adequately conducted research that answers a large chunk of their inquiry questions,

Table 3.4 Possible Digital Tools for Stage One Implementation

Mentimeter	Enter ideas or answers into a word cloud that shows the most common results
Poll Everywhere	Initial ideas about a challenge are tabulated
Popplet	Mind-map thinking and learning to generate solutions and plan projects
Coggle.it	Graphically organize an approach to a challenge

they move into the development, testing, and refinement of their solution ideas. Of course, this part of the journey is cyclical as they try out options that may or may not work. Sometimes, they literally must go back to the drawing board. Explore the digital tools in Table 3.5 to envision how you might enhance the learning experience in Stage Two.

> **Stage Three: Context and Perspective**
>
> How do we know if our learners have considered end-user needs and technical expert feedback?

Even though our learners may have the research and data to support their initial ideas to effectively solve the challenge, it is necessary that they pause to consider other options on the subject. Feedback from technical experts is one of the most essential components of the authentic challenge process. Now, our learners gain valuable insight from a person or persons who are professionals in the area of study that relates to the challenge. This feedback then serves as a way for our learners and us to determine if they need to reenter Stage Two for additional inquiry, research, and refinement. Of course, as we have already noted in previous chapters when our technical experts are not available for an in-person session, technology serves to bridge the divide between sites so that all of our learners, no matter their location, have the opportunity to engage in this critical aspect of the learning and development process.

Moreover, as our learners often find themselves in a geographically isolated bubble, of sorts, these online connections become even more valuable. This stage is also the perfect time to compare your learners' context of the challenge to any peers from different areas of their state and country to beyond their geographic boundaries. As we expose our learners to different backgrounds and cultures, our learners will grow as empathetic citizens, and they will begin to comprehend better the complexity of the challenge based on their contextual understandings.

Table 3.5 Possible Digital Tools for Stage Two Implementation

Backchannel Chat	Use to share thoughts/questions about a technical expert speaker for review in real time or later
WebJets	Create online boards with embedded video, files, links, etc. and organize them into folders
Kahoot	Share learning with the whole class
Google Docs	Collaborate and compile gathered research and data

As our learners consider these multiple perspectives from peers and technical experts, the sum of their proposal increases exponentially. Collaborative technologies open the doors for new networks to materialize that strengthen future connections for our learners. These networks that our learners build during a challenge can lead to job opportunities in the future. Explore the digital tools in Table 3.6 to envision how you might enhance the learning experience in Stage Three.

> **Stage Four: Actions and Consequences**
>
> How do we know if our learners have considered the potential positive and negative impacts of their proposed solution?

One of the easiest ways to get our learners to understand that there are consequences to their actions is to have them consider what occurs when they take the ideas of others and call them their own. Of course, if you design an entirely open-ended question for your learners to tackle, this dramatically decreases the possibility that they could pass off another's idea as their own, unlike the totem pole example I discussed in Chapter 2. However, since our learners must delve into the inquiry process in Stage Two, they will gather research to help them develop their ideas. Thus, it is necessary for them to cite their sources as they review the potential positive and negative outcomes of their proposed solution. The citation of these sources justifies their answers and makes them more acceptable.

It is much easier to look at a whole system than it is to break the system down into parts. A complete system is a surface-level view. Conversely, if our learners break a problem down into segmented pieces, they must view the interplay between each component from a much more complex vantage point. Each part then relates to a potential positive or negative consequence of their proposed solution. Our learners must articulate these possible consequences and review how they intend to combat those that are negative and highlight those that are positive.

Table 3.6 Possible Digital Tools for Stage Three Implementation

Notability	Learners combine handwriting, photos, and typed annotations to share their project solutions and receive feedback
Equity Maps	Keep track of participation in whole class feedback sessions or Socratic Seminars
Flip Grid	Provide feedback via videos
Kaizena	Embed voice comments into Google Docs

As our learners begin to realize there are both positive and negative possibilities that may result as an implication of the implementation of their solution, they must conduct a cost–benefit analysis of that solution. Ultimately, the benefits must outweigh the costs, and our learners must determine how they can minimize those costs. Furthermore, our learners must figure out how to mitigate these costs as they communicate their solutions. The platform and tools they choose to use as they achieve their objective directly affect how their audience will receive their proposed ideas. Explore the digital tools in Table 3.7 to envision how you might enhance the learning experience in Stage Four.

> **Stage Five: Options and Opportunities**
>
> How do we know if our learners have developed an actionable solution for their end-users?

The end-user is the essential consideration our learners must have when designing an appropriate solution to the challenge. What works for one group of users in one context won't necessarily work for another group. Therefore, our learners must showcase a meaningful connection between their solution and their intended, collective end-user. As such, it is vital that our learners share the process of how they came to their presented conclusion. A documented curation of the learning process and its evolution goes a long way in convincing their audience that the solution is workable for their end-user group. One of the easiest ways to curate the information is through an online journal or blog. Before our learners even get to Stage Five, this online journal can serve as a feedback opportunity from technical experts, their peers, and you. This journal also serves as a documentation of their learning journey.

Open-ended, authentic project-based learning experiences are not a quick endeavor. While I have witnessed some successful year-long projects, I wouldn't recommend starting here. However, depending on the length of your class periods, you can expect to spend two to three weeks, on average, for any given

Table 3.7 Possible Digital Tools for Stage Four Implementation

Primary Pad	Engage in an online discussion with a small group that allows the teacher to monitor multiple conversations at once
360 Cities	Experience a total immersion into a city to think about how the solution might impact the area
NewsMap	Google News Aggregator to reflect on positive and negative possibilities
Roambi Analytics	Create spreadsheets on a mobile device to conduct a cost–benefit analysis

project. Some can certainly go longer and this is dependent on the scope of the content and the number of standards included in the project.

To help you consider the length of the project implementation, I like to share with teachers what I call my 10 percent rule. The math is simple, as you determine how many traditional lesson days a unit of study might take you to complete, and then you add 10 percent onto those days to give you the total number of days you can afford to dedicate to the learning experience. For the ease of math, let's use a base of ten. Therefore, I can spend as many as eleven days on a project but not twelve, thirteen, or more. Generally speaking, this rule provides me with plenty of time to implement all of my units, as PBL, with a few days allotted to spend for any other miscellaneous topic I might want to include that doesn't fit well within the scope of a project.

Since our learners might be spending a considerable amount of time on a project, we very well may need to ensure they have the stamina to do so. While I am not a fan of the word grit, and I certainly don't like to use the phrase "failing forward," there is a need to support our learners. When they waiver or falter during the process, as the ambiguity that is part of the challenge can be unnerving for our learners, we must support them. Ultimately, the time is well spent, however, as our learners present their actionable solution to their audience in Stage Five.

Sometimes, we know precisely who our intended audience is for the challenge and the where and how of the showcase plans for sharing the learning. However, this is not always the case as we enter into the challenge. It is conceivable that we might want our learners to make that determination. Thus, the content and how our learners present the solution is a critical consideration for our learners. Consider the situation in which we invite a panel of experts into the classroom versus one in which our learners must go out into the community to connect with their audience. Indeed, the latter is a higher level of intensity for our learners, and the professionalism of the presentation should match the venue. For example, if PowerPoint slides are part of the presentation to share charts and graphs that support the solution (not to share fifty words per slide that your learners read directly), the background of the slides must not affect the projection of them negatively. A white background is preferable, as other colors and busy templates do not translate well from the computer screen to the projection screen.

While our venue is a consideration for Stage Five, so, too, is the message that we share. Just as our ELA educators ensure our learners know how to write for differing purposes, so must we guarantee our learners are ready to interact with their audience with a tailored message for them. A great way to have your learners practice this message is to complete a sound bite on their topic. In twenty-seven words, nine seconds, and with three thoughts, they should be able to convince their audience to buy into their proposed solution. While the actual presentation, if it is, in fact, a formal presentation, will be much longer than this, the sound bite is the perfect way to have your learners practice being concise and to the point. If your learners don't intend to give a formal presentation, you can still use this method to help your learners focus their message.

Finally, it is necessary for your learners to choose the best way to connect with their audience. While a presentation might be the way to go for some projects, other times, a presentation may not even be a consideration due to the nature of the audience or the goals of the project. Therefore, early on, in Stage Two or Three, if your learners have the option to decide their medium, they will want to do so then. By Stage Five, this should be a solid conclusion as to how your learners want to share the solution with the audience as the best method to communicate their message. Explore the digital tools in Table 3.8 to envision how you might enhance the learning experience in Stage Five.

An Example Project Aligned to the ISTE Standards for Students

Now that we have linked our ISTE standards for students to our Five Project Assessment Stages let's review an example project. This project exhibits the ISTE standards for students authentically and complexly and supports our learners to meet all of the criteria for our five stages. As you read through the project, jot down notes on how the project answers our five assessment questions.

Marsh Creek Sixth-Grade Center, in Downingtown, Pennsylvania, the summer before it opened, decided they needed to find a way to connect its 1,200 preteens in a way that would bring them together as a community when they were, in actuality, from various townships within the district. With learners from eight municipalities and ten elementary schools, it was essential to the principal, Tom Mulvey, and his staff, who were also shifting to a new building, to create a Marsh Creek community. Thus, the planning began to develop an art and identity signature project that would do just that. The challenge was posed to every sixth-grader: "How can we use art to define who we are as individuals,

Table 3.8 Possible Digital Tools for Stage Five Implementation

VoiceThread	Possible presentation option that allows for online interaction between the presenter and the audience
FreshGrade	Curate and share work as a digital portfolio
QR Codes	Share interactive stories behind a shared artifact
Google Tour Creator	Create a tour of an area using Google street images or your own 360 photos

a community, and agents of change?" Since art was the central part of this challenge, art teacher, Laura Roth, took the helm of this massive undertaking. She enlisted the help of the social studies, English language arts, and instructional design and information technology departments to design and implement the project. From the cross-collaborative experience, not only would the new Marsh Creek community be defined but also how the learners, as individuals, could be agents of change in the world would push the boundaries of what eleven- and twelve-year-old learners could do to effect change.

The project started with a visit from the curator of the West Collection. (The West Collection is a group of Philadelphia contemporary art installations.) Learners were able to vote on the artwork they wanted to borrow as part of a mobile art gallery display for their school. From here, learners began their investigation into how they would answer the challenge. Through this, learners individually developed a multimedia composition of art that displayed them as individuals in the foreground of the piece, established how they were part of the community in the middle ground of the piece, and how they could be an agent of change in the background of the piece. Essays were written in ELA class and then recorded to explain how the students saw themselves as part of the community and as agents of change. These recordings linked to the art pieces through a QR code. Finally, the social studies classes supported this work as they led their learners on a historic discovery of communities and change agents. These were used to inform the decisions for their art creations and accompanying essays. The finished products resulted in a local TEDx talk on art and identity and an art fair in which all 1,200 art pieces received a display throughout the entire Downingtown community. In fact, Ms. Roth personally shipped several dozen of the chosen art pieces to the State Capitol in Harrisburg for a special two-week showing.

This exemplary project is a testament to how a group of educators can collaborate to enrich the lives of their learners. Throughout this educational journey, these sixth-graders were empowered to define who they are as individuals and as a part of a greater school community. As they created their individual art pieces and the stories behind them, they had the opportunity to construct and make meaning of the newfound knowledge in a variety of cross-curricular components, as they designed an innovative way to showcase their identity as a learner. The art itself was a creative way to communicate the global impacts of their learning. The incorporation of the technology tools in such a way not typically leveraged in art classes exhibited digital citizenship and computational thinking that these learners are sure to carry with them into middle school and beyond.

Sometimes it is easier to consider how we might align our skills-based standards from this chapter to our authentic challenge than it is to think about our content standards from Chapter 2. If you struggled with ideas after reading the last chapter, perhaps you now feel more confident about your potential design. If you need to, feel free to go back and review the ideas in Chapter 2 before moving on to Chapter 4. In any case, no matter what degree of technology tools you and your learners have at your disposal, instructional technology can help you to rewrite the educational journey on which you and your learners embark.

Time to Reflect
1. How does your project idea align to the overarching ISTE Standards for Students?
2. How do the sub-standards for the ISTE Standards for Students propel your project idea into a more authentic, relevant, and complex challenge?
3. How do your content standards become more meaningful when you align them to skills-based standards?
Record Any Questions You Have Here

4

Generate Authentic Reading and Writing

> How can I support the development of my learners as better readers and writers through the implementation of authentic learning experiences?

When was your love for reading defined? I distinctly remember my discovery of the Nancy Drew series in third or fourth grade, which began my never-ending need to have a new mystery on hand. In the summer before seventh grade, I won the reading contest by finishing over a hundred books. There was never a time I wasn't reading. However, I cannot seem to recall a time in which I wanted to read for school. My memories of reading in school are limited to textbooks and encyclopedias, as my tenure as a student in the K–12 system was a few years before the World Wide Web allowed us to update content as history occurs. As for writing, again, I am at a loss for when I was required to write more than a few sentences before high school began. Although, I know I dreaded my weekly spelling word sentences. If you had told preteen Dayna that she would grow up to be the author of multiple books, she probably would not have believed you!

What educator doesn't want their learners to get lost in a complex tangle of words in a story, intrigued by an unusual phenomenon that paints a picture with words that jump off the page, and excited by the prospect of changing the world by the words they write? The way our older children can get lost in a story that transforms fiction into a vibrant world of fantasy or the excitement that exudes from a child who has learned a surprising new fact brings us boundless joy. But, all too frequently, we know how we have learners who shut down when it comes to reading. For those children who struggled in their early elementary years, they are now behind the ball for literacy success. It is even more disheartening for our young middle learners that continue to falter in their reading comprehension.

So much of what our learners must accomplish is tied to reading and writing. This literacy achievement is especially significant in the later elementary school years to ensure we prepare our learners to tackle more difficult texts and write for a defined purpose. In middle school, it is imperative our learners gain a deeper appreciation for reading both fiction and nonfiction and develop a desire to express themselves through writing. This appreciation prepares them to become better-informed learners throughout their adult lives.

Unfortunately, and all too frequently, reading becomes a struggle at school and at home around the fourth grade. As the complexities of the texts increase with each grade level, the more likely it is that our struggling readers will shut down. Moreover, with an intensification in the demand of writing for both length and purpose, far more learners begin to avoid writing whenever possible. We want to shift these trends and bring meaning to what our learners read and write, so they acquire the skills that have the power to bring about excitement for literacy.

The desire for our learners to embrace reading fiction and nonfiction is a major goal for all educators. The evidence of our learners' abilities to interpret, evaluate, and communicate the meaning of content and its impact on the world around them is paramount as we prepare them for middle or high school. Moreover, as the call for writing intensifies in length, skill, and expectation, the purpose for that writing plays an integral part in the buy-in of that writing assignment for our learners. Here, authentic challenges provide the space for our learners to make meaning out of what they read and bring relevance to what they write. As we strengthen our learners' aptitudes for reading and writing, we enhance their abilities to explore, uncover, and solve challenges.

How can I support the development of my learners as better readers and writers through the implementation of authentic learning experiences? The parallel between projects and literacy is not limited to an ELA classroom. Our text selections and writing assignments have the potential to tap into the agile learners we desire to cultivate in our classrooms, no matter what age and grade level. It isn't unusual, however, for teachers to express the following concerns as they begin to explore authentic project-based learning:

- I have required texts that I have to teach, and I'm not sure how they fit into a project.
- I'm not an ELA teacher and don't have time to teach reading and writing.
- Many of my learners don't have the level of reading and writing skills necessary to participate in an authentic project.
- My classroom full of learners is so varied in reading and writing ability that I'm not sure how to meet the needs of all of my learners through a project.
- I am unsure what texts I might use that could correspond to an authentic project.

Using a project-based learning pedagogy creates a relevant avenue for our learners to explore literacy in our content area even if we are not ELA teachers. (Remember, the Common Core State Standards push for the use of nonfiction texts in 70 percent of what our students read. Subsequently, all non-ELA teachers must incorporate a great deal of literacy into their classroom strategies.) Since literacy skills are foundational for completing meaningful research, we must think about the scaffolding process to support the development of these skills within our learners. These incorporated scaffolds guide our learners toward innovating actionable solutions that meet the needs of their end-users. Thus, we see the need to incorporate literacy into our projects at every stage.

Recall, there is a need to establish a purpose for the authentic challenge at its start. While we may take our learners on a local or virtual field trip, bring in a guest speaker, or view a compelling video clip, books and other engaging informational texts are an added opportunity to provide the launching point for our challenge. A literacy launch can also invite our learners into the inquiry process and help them to define the relevant purpose behind the challenge. From these readings, our learners immediately begin to document their connections between the challenge and the stories and pictures painted by the words they read. These texts are undoubtedly enhanced when we incorporate charts, graphs, and other visual aids that serve as illustrative interpretations of the written texts. Additionally, these are the same books, articles, or primary source documents they may use later during guided reading, in upper elementary or ELA class. In our other middle school courses, more complex readings can also be used to spark known connections to the challenge. The more descriptive the text, the deeper the connections potentially run. The personal links to the chosen reading push our learners deeper into the inquiry phenomena. To illustrate the importance of this inquiry, let's take a look at a multi-grade example that could launch a challenge using stories to spark relevant inquiry questions.

To bring your kids into the conversation rather than tell them what the challenge should entail, read several of the stories from Sundem's *Real Kids, Real Stories, Real Change: Courageous Actions Around the World.* Depending on your grade level and content area, you can pick and choose which story or stories to read. This particular book provides a variety of launching points for inquiry and has a wonderful way of connecting with young people. While the destruction of the Central American rainforest may not hit close to home, your learners could connect with Omar's long walk to save it and might consider actions they could take for an issue closer to home. Similarly, while Henry worked to protect the turtles whose habitats were threatened by a new housing project, your learners might not see an immediate association to reptiles. However, I guarantee there are many other species that they could connect to on a local level. Conversely, when Ryan invents a sign language translator in an effort to get a date, your older middle school teens might just be intrigued immediately.

Each story in the *Real Kids* book provides curricular connections from multiple vantage points. Science abounds in the turtle example, as we think about the destruction of habitats and even the extinction of species. Social studies also links to this example through public policy and civic duty. Moreover, ELA and writing could serve as a foundational component for any writing for an actionable change. We can even bring in math with statistical data analysis, graphing, and linear equations. It is up to you which content area you prefer to be the anchor for the challenge. If you teach at the upper elementary level, you may find it easy to integrate the different content areas you teach. If you are at the middle school level and have a collaborative and supportive team, it is conceivable that all four content areas could establish a challenge from any of these ideas. Therefore, I encourage you to seek out this book as an inspiration to you and your learners.

The Common Core State Standards (CCSS), or your specific state standards (TEKS, SOLs, etc.), have a direct focus on literacy skills. As previously mentioned, according to the CCSS, 70 percent of what learners are to read is nonfiction text. I believe the designers of the standards specifically engineered them in this way to encourage educators of all disciplines to make literacy more of a priority. Moreover, additional national standards such as the C3 Social Studies Framework align well to literacy as we incorporate a variety of primary and secondary sources for evaluation in Stages Two and Three.

Literacy steeped in nonfiction is especially vital, as nonfiction texts bombard us daily as we complete our jobs or read the latest news. Of course, this does not mean that fiction is limited to select units in an ELA classroom. Instead, we can utilize our fiction texts as case studies related to the challenge. While we delve into this case study potential in a bit more detail later on in this chapter, for now let's tie it to my *Real Kids* example from above. While the *Real Kids* book is a nonfiction case study, you can also seek out fiction examples to relate to any of the topic challenges. A fiction text would have enhanced their understanding from a very different perspective than merely using a nonfiction text. While this, of course, is not a requirement, it is up to each teacher to determine. Furthermore, the development of a cross-curricular experience allows for additional literacy components such as this.

There is a compilation of possible authentic learning experiences aligned to a variety of national standards in Chapter 2. Refer back to Table 2.4 and imagine the possibilities for direct literacy connections to those examples. After trying this on your own, compare your ideas to the list of possible extensions in Table 4.1 for several of those projects. Please note, for simplification purposes, I have only provided one standard with each example. Other standards, however, are applicable.

Whether we focus on a science project, social studies project, math project, or a project for any of our other specialty content areas, literacy is a thread that weaves the connections between the content areas. While this may be more difficult to comprehend for middle school teachers who are generally subject-specific, we must not forget the importance of these literacy connections. We don't all have to teach fiction from the perspective of symbolism or themes, but we must all teach reading and writing with our content area as the appropriate lens. Make the reading, writing, listening, and speaking standards the foundation of your challenge from which you build the supports via any other content area you desire. This foundation is how we can make our other core content areas authentic.

When we make literacy a foundational component of our project, the reading and writing now have a purpose for our learners. Rather than reading for a predetermined number of minutes or writing about a preselected topic chosen by the state, our learners have the opportunity to grow as both readers and writers as they are empowered to potentially effect change in their world. Our authentic challenges provide our learners with the opportunity to interact with nonfiction text selections purposefully. This purpose moves our learners beyond simply reading an often-outdated textbook to take outlined notes or answer the questions at the end of the section.

Table 4.1 Standards Aligned to Authentic Literacy Projects

Standard	Authentic Challenge	Literacy Connection
CCSS.ELA.RI.8.1. Cite the textual evidence that most strongly supports an analysis of what the text says explicitly as well as inferences drawn from the text.	Write a bill proposal on a topic relevant to your community that includes statistical data analysis and present the plan to your local congressman.	♦ Read *Helping Hands* to ignite ideas on how to connect to the community ♦ Read *Pay It Forward (Young Reader's Edition)* to envision how helping others can go beyond one or two persons to effect change as a whole.
CCSS.ELA.RL.4.5. Explain major differences between poems, drama, and prose, and refer to the structural elements of poems and drama when writing or speaking about a text.	Submit an original poem or editorial to a local news or community publication linked to a studied topic in social studies.	♦ Read *The Death of the Hat: A Brief History of Poetry in 50 Objects* to inspire how poetry can link to history. ♦ Read *How to Eat a Poem* to inspire learners from a variety of poets throughout the ages.
CCSS.ELA.RL.6.4. Determine the meaning of words and phrases as they are used in a text, including figurative and connotative meanings; analyze the impact of a specific word choice on meaning and tone.	Develop a plan to reduce food waste in the cafeteria, or extend the plan to the community and beyond.	♦ Read *It's Disgusting and We Ate It! True Food Facts from Around the World and Throughout History* to engage kids in the idea that food is both revered and wasted. ♦ Read *What a Waste! Where Does Garbage Go?* to get kids thinking about the impact of the waste they generate.
CCSS.ELA.5.7. Draw on information from multiple print or digital sources, demonstrating the ability to locate an answer to a question quickly or to solve a problem efficiently.	Develop a student-run business for the school with a required business plan to be presented to district administration for approval. Small business owners from the community provide feedback through the development process.	♦ Read *Kid Start-Up: How You Can Be an Entrepreneur* to have kids start to list the qualities necessary to be a successful entrepreneur. ♦ Read *Kid Millionaire: Over 50 Exciting Business Ideas* to have kids start to brainstorm ideas for a viable business.

Now, our learners have the occasion to engage with multiple nonfiction texts and at a variety of reading levels. Since we know we have a range of reading level capabilities within our classroom, it is vital that we provide multiple options for texts when appropriate. If you have access to your readers' Lexile scores, this is the perfect time to analyze this data. You can challenge your more advanced readers with Google Scholar and partner with your reading specialists to find appropriate level texts for your struggling readers. If you have access to NetTrekker, I encourage you to use this as a resource for leveled texts. While it is not a free service, it is a highly valuable one. Educators vet all of the sources posted, and each reading has an accompanying Lexile score attached to it. Now, your readers can search for a text that is at the appropriate level for them. They can also challenge themselves to choose a text at one level higher than they might usually read, as they feel comfortable.

The exposure to an array of texts is especially critical to ensure our learners don't feign boredom with the subject due to a lack of comprehension and fluency skills. When our learners read an informational piece that contains a plethora of unfamiliar academic or content-specific vocabulary, it can be overwhelming. Thus, it is essential to link the text back to an authentic purpose for reading. Additionally, a purpose for the reading grounds the learner in the context of the project such that they make such connections from the start. This desired connection means we have to shift from traditional vocabulary lessons such as merely defining words, and we must start to embed scaffolding strategies that support the acquisition of new or unfamiliar vocabulary. These strategies might include a GLAD (Guided Language Acquisition Design) strategy such as the Cognitive Content Dictionary in which learners predict the meaning of the word, write or sketch something that helps them remember the word, and then use the word in a sentence. Another digital strategy that works here is the use of Lexipedia in which the tool indicates parts of speech with color-codes, as well as relationships between words. Thus, as we give our learners numerous chances to engage with new vocabulary and content, we increase their ability to go beyond the mere retention of definitions as the new terms now connect to a relevant purpose. This is the point at which our learners begin to use the new vocabulary in an authentic and conversational context. Through this process, we start to see a voracious attitude toward reading and the desire to consume more information related to the challenge as our learners begin to formulate their potential solution ideas.

While nonfiction works naturally lend themselves to authentic challenges, we also have the opportunity to embed works of fiction into the mix. For those of you who are ELA teachers, use the authentic challenge to connect to a literary character. If your district requires a whole class novel, think about the intersection of the story with real life. What are the parallels? Consider how you can use these parallels with character development as a case study for the challenge. And, for those of you who are not ELA teachers, what stories relate to your content? Of course, history and ELA often naturally align as settings of novels are frequently linked to a historical era. However, science can be viewed through stories, as well. Think about Dr. Seuss's *The Lorax*, which has layers of complexity that we could peel back and make appropriate for a variety of grade levels when studying the environment. Or, for ten to twelve year olds, you might choose something such as *The Misfits No. 4: The Kingfisher's Tale* or *Fuzzy Mud*. For upper middle school, *Girlwood* would be an excellent choice.

Literacy is, however, more than reading. While some of our learners are good readers and need little prompting to dive into a text, either fiction or nonfiction, some of those same learners do not naturally excel at writing. Arguably, the more a learner reads, the more their writing improves. Writing, therefore, is the long-term process that guides our learners to turn their ideas into viable solutions and well-developed stories (Laur & Ackers, 2017). Since writing is the foundation for our challenges, we must include it at each project stage as frequently as possible. These writing opportunities are formative assessments that help us to make adjustments to our instructions. Moreover, they document the process of learning as we watch each learner grow in the complexity of their solution and articulate the justification of their reasoning. This document should also include how their perspectives of the challenge have evolved and the changes they have made to their ideas over time. These writing reflections now have purpose and meaning for our learners.

Not long ago, I had a principal comment that she couldn't figure out how to increase her school's writing scores on the state test. The lack of improvement confounded her even with all of the writing strategies her teachers had adopted and implemented. Immediately, I responded with, "Have you provided your learners with a purpose for their writing?" Her response was not surprising: "Well, of course, it is to do well on the test!" Unfortunately, for her, that wasn't a meaningful purpose for the majority of her school population.

Authentic challenges provide our learners with a reason to write and to do so for an authentic audience. Learners who engage in writing for a purpose must use diverse genres of writing to communicate their solutions and the justification for those solutions (Laur & Ackers, 2017). As such, not only do I encourage you to use writing as frequently as possible throughout the project, but I also urge you to vary the types of writing you ask of your learners as they consider their targeted authentic audience. This means a summative writing product is an important component of the project. Therefore, the writing tone is likely to shift from narrative to informational to persuasive at various points throughout the project. Now, as non-ELA teachers, you are supporting your ELA colleagues, while those of you who are ELA teachers have created more of a direct purpose and relevance for the reading and writing tasks asked of your learners.

To improve your learners' writing abilities, you must intentionally focus on writing as it supports your content and standards. At this point in your journey, for those of you who are upper elementary teachers, you may still separate reading and writing into designated times of the day or maybe you have started to integrate them into your other content areas. For those of you in the middle grades, I hope you have reconsidered the segmenting of reading and writing into a stand-alone ELA class. The dedication of a portion of your class period to writing gives your learners the facilitated space to build and strengthen the academic vocabulary needed in the challenge. Writing is another opportunity to practice the authentic challenge vocabulary words. Now, rather than simply remembering a definition of a vocabulary word or memorizing how to spell them for the weekly spelling test, our learners have a purpose to provide meaning and context to the words through their writing. Whether they draft a proposal to implement change or craft an opinion piece supporting their solution, the use of vocabulary words strengthens the required writing and provides you with the opportunity to assess their understanding of the content (Laur & Ackers, 2017).

As our learners progress through an authentic challenge, Bloom's Taxonomy offers us a structure to support reading and writing at each level. As our learners answer the challenge question at the creation level, we provide a broader foundation to support the acquisition and mastery of their written and spoken language through the lower levels of Bloom's. Here, you may wish to refer to Table 4.2 (adapted from Laur & Ackers, 2017) for examples of how to align your approach to literacy with Bloom's.

The early part of this chapter started with concerns I inherently know many of you have. Hopefully, some of those concerns have been alleviated to some degree. However, you are probably also wondering about what this looks like in your classrooms. As you move into this next section on how literacy supports each Stage of Project Assessment notice how each day or class period offers lesson ideas and activities that support literacy development. These offerings should be predicated on the formative assessments (Chapter 5) you complete. Thus, use this section as a sample guide. Your challenge may play out differently than what I have described here.

Literacy in Stage One of Project Assessment

Challenge and Purpose

How do we know if our learners understand and are invested in the challenge?

2–3 days

Table 4.2 Bloom's Alignment to Literacy

Bloom's	Reading	Writing and Speaking
Creating	1. Rewrite the ending to a story related to the challenge topic 2. Compile an anthology of primary source documents that support the challenge solution	1. Written proposal or editorial supporting the final idea 2. Compile an original anthology of poems or short stories
Evaluating	1. Evaluate the information contained in a primary source versus a secondary source 2. Compare sources to determine similarities and differences	1. Debate, in a small or large group, the merits of a possible solution to the challenge 2. Write an essay comparing the potential value of the sum of the proposed solutions
Analyzing	1. Analyze the character development as a case study related to the challenge 2. Determine the author's perspective as it relates to the challenge	1. Complete a Venn Diagram comparing a personal journal entry with a peer's entry as related to the challenge question 2. Explain the theory behind the results of initial idea testing with a technical expert
Applying	1. Answer pre/post-reading questions related to the processing of new information and making personal connections 2. Engage in hands-on activities, experiments, and labs that guide learners to connect and apply project vocabulary and information	1. Write out and describe the steps they wish to take on how to create their final products 2. Write questions for and conduct an interview of a technical expert on the topic challenge
Understanding	1. Recognize texts as primary versus secondary sources and fiction versus nonfiction 2. Restate the story in own words	1. Restate the challenge in their own words as a journaling assignment 2. Explain to a peer the importance of the challenge
Remembering	1. Reading response and reflection discussions 2. Vocabulary development through project-related texts	1. Vocabulary development through written definitions 2. Prepare a "What I Learned" presentation for a small group

Day One of Stage One

At the start of our project, we have the opportunity to practice and refine literacy skills. When we introduce the challenge, we must engage our learners from the start. As previously mentioned, while we have the option to launch with a fantastic field trip or dynamic guest speaker, among other possibilities, we might merely connect to a reading. As offered as an example in Table 4.1, our learners read *The Death of the Hat: A Brief History of Poetry in 50 Objects* to immediately connect them with the ways in which ordinary objects can inspire poetry. After our learners have thought about the challenge, we provide them with quiet reflection time on the problem to list any questions they might have about the challenge. I call this the inquiry list and, it is quite literally the beginning of the inquiry process that goes much deeper in Stage Two.

If this is your first foray into inquiry in this manner, this may be the first indication that your learners are not used to asking questions. It is natural for them to want to know the answer to the challenge immediately. However, when we provide them with time to think and encourage them to write down any and all questions they might have about the challenge, the results are outstanding. For some of your learners who are new to project-based learning or for your learners who need additional support due to an IEP, 504 Plan or language barriers, feel free to require a certain number of questions. The more frequently your learners participate in this process, the higher the number of questions they are likely to develop. For example, you may start with three questions, while your advanced learners could fill an entire page with possible questions.

As your learners become more advanced in this practice, you can vary how you ask them to ideate their initial inquiry questions. Some teachers prefer to use the Question Formulation Technique, while others like the Breakdown Strategy that requires learners first to list the anticipated steps to complete the challenge before moving into compiling the questions for each step. This first day is also the perfect time to try my version of the Socratic Seminar discussed in Appendix 1. No matter what method you opt to try, each one produces the questions needed to move on to Stage Two in a few days. Just remember to start the formulation of questions on an individual basis before moving into small groups and, eventually, the full class. The individual approach provides us with a pre-assessment of our learners' understanding of the challenge.

Day Two of Stage One

Start this class period with a written model of the connection between the inquiry questions to map the ideas associated with the challenge. Of course, a concept or mind map works well here as a scaffold before a complete articulation of the connection in paragraph form. Again, this is an excellent formative assessment of our learners' understanding of the problem.

Once you feel confident that your learners are ready to move forward, establish a series of anchor charts around your classroom or digitally, if you prefer. Your learners should be in charge of determining what topics belong on the charts. And, they can start to add small bits of known information to them. I suggest, at this juncture, post-it notes for the information additions.

Since we are early in this challenge process, it is possible a misinformed learner will add a post-it that is non-germane to the challenge or just a misinterpretation of the problem.

Day Three of Stage One

If you have teams of learners working on the challenge now is the time to get them into their groups. Rather than have my learners develop a contract for how their team intended to move forward, I prefer to have them write a story of their learning as they predict it will emerge throughout the challenge. A protocol such as the National School Reform Faculty's "Back to the Future" works well here. For this, a modified approach fits well with time constraints. Learners collectively, rather than individually, craft in present tense language a future projection of what the best case scenario is for solving the challenge. Then, learners use past tense wording to describe how their work on the challenge started. Finally, learners use past tense vocabulary to discuss how they moved from the starting place and into the future.

The use of a protocol such as this, as opposed to a contract, makes the work actionable for our learners. Rather than produce an agreement that has mostly meaningless language such as "we promise to listen to each other's ideas," now, they have something tangible to work toward throughout the project. While there might still be hiccups along the way in how your teams function, you can always bring them back to this writing to revisit and revise, addressing how they solved the team dysfunction.

Literacy in Stage Two of Project Assessment

> **Inquiry and Ideas**
>
> How do we know if our learners have explored multiple pathways to a solution?
>
> 3–8 days

Day One of Stage Two

Once we have established the purpose of their challenge and our learners understand it and are excited about it, it is time to start to research and gather data. Our learners already have a list of inquiry questions they generated during the first day of the challenge. We use these questions to have our learners begin the research process individually. This individuality helps with the formative assessment discussed in Chapter 5. Moreover, it ensures that research skills have the potential to be equally developed by everyone. Here, they start to collect information via databases, interviews, surveys, or field trips (virtual or on site).

It is advisable to begin the research for your learners, or you can tap into your librarian for assistance. By this, I mean you have the opportunity to compile a list of starting points for them to investigate. This is needed as research can take longer than time allows. By designating a sound list of sources, you effectively ensure your learners will not immediately stray down a path that isn't an efficient use of their time. Of course, you don't want to limit your learners to this list and should expect additional sources to accompany their research.

Days Two, Three, and Four of Stage Two

I like to use Diigo as an online sharing tool to compile these sources. Diigo also allows learners to highlight and annotate the text in an online "talking to the text" approach. For us, as teachers, we can also track any comments as a formative assessment. For our learners, if teamed, they can share their comments with the group to create a more dynamic reference point as they begin to generate their initial ideas for the solution to the challenge. However, any online tool that is preferred can house the compiled research. Google Docs is an acceptable online tool that also eliminates the issue of an absent learner who may have taken the research home the night before.

Through this research, our learners also continue to generate additional inquiry questions and can add to the anchor charts. However, once the initial investigation is exhausted, it is time for our learners to produce their first ideas for the solution to the challenge. This idea generation is, again, done on an individual basis to allow for that all-important formative assessment.

Day Five of Stage Two

Project teams, if you have them, are ready to meet once their initial ideas are on paper or recorded digitally. As our teams meet, they must bring a portion of a text they have selected that helps to justify their shared, initial idea. Teams then conduct a "Three Levels of Text" protocol, also developed by the National School Reform Faculty. Before sharing their solution idea, a learner completes the first level of the protocol by reading their selected text passage. In the second level of the protocol, the learner explains their interpretation of the passage and why it resonated with them. Finally, in the third level of the protocol, the learner discusses how this passage made an implication on the development of their idea. All members of the team repeat this process.

From this protocol, we now have a team with numerous ideas that are grounded in sound inquiry. All team members share an idea with equal weight, and all of the ideas have the potential to move forward. From here, it is time for the individual ideas to be rated and, if necessary, combined. To determine which idea or combination of ideas is appropriate for further development, any number of protocols is appropriate. The NUF test, discussed in more detail in Chapter 7, is one possibility. A rating score on whether the idea is new, useful, and feasible helps the team to pick an idea on which they will focus. Another possible protocol to utilize is the GRASPS method, an *Understanding by Design* concept (Wiggins & McTighe, 2004). From this, our learners must identify the solution's real-world connection to the goal, role, audience, situation, product/performance, and standards to be met with the implementation of the proposed solution. In either of these examples, our learners have a more targeted way of determining the best possible solution as a team decision. Feel free to look at Appendix 1 for additional protocols that are appropriate for this idea sharing stage.

Days Six and Seven of Stage Two

As these individual and original thoughts meld into a team-developed solution throughout the remainder of this stage, our learners continue to engage in inquiry as they read additional texts and books. It is certainly appropriate, here, to guide our learners as we provide assistance in identifying and locating research materials. As our learners read layers of text that answer their inquiry questions, they begin to uncover needed modifications to their initial ideas without our direct input. Furthermore, this is the opportune time for our learners to conduct a survey that targets their end-user audience or is designed to elicit information regarding a similar situation that may inform their own idea development. This data serves to enhance the support of their idea or will cause our learners to make additional modifications. We can assess the progress of individual and team idea development as our learners use their writing skills to document the development of their ideas via Google Docs or any other platform of your choice. Additionally, reflecting on the challenge question is appropriate to gauge how our learners have evolved in their idea development and modifications. I like to use this method as a daily journaling opportunity.

Day Eight of Stage Two

Before we move into the more formal stage for feedback, now is the time for informal, peer feedback. The presentation of initial ideas can take the form of a class gallery walk or any other presentation method you choose

(Laur & Ackers, 2017). This day also provides the perfect chance to complete a SWOT analysis. The strengths, weaknesses, opportunities, and threats are determined in this analysis protocol. To enhance the effectiveness of it, try having your teams complete a SWOT analysis on their own work, and then have them compare it to a SWOT analysis that another team completes for their idea. It is up to you how many SWOT analyses you want to require from each team. Effectively, you can have as few as two (own team and one other team) or as many as there are total teams. Now, as our teams start to shift into Stage Three, our learners begin to think about feedback in a variety of forms.

Literacy in Stage Three of Project Assessment

> **Context and Perspective**
>
> How do we know if our learners have considered end-user needs and technical expert feedback?
>
> 2–4 days

Day One of Stage Three

To ensure our learners have not lost sight of the context of the challenge, as they enter into this stage, now is an excellent time to reinforce the context through literacy. The use of the Literacy TA strategy, I Know/You Know (see Appendix 1 for details), is something you may want to try as a support. For this, be sure to mix up teams of learners with a partner to get a variety of perspectives. You can also do several rounds, as the timing on this one is relatively short at 30 seconds per round with four rounds in total in a pairing. While you can adjust the timing to a minute or slightly longer, I suggest aiming for the short timeframe after your learners feel comfortable with the protocol. This limited time structure causes your learners to be very concise.

Another option at this stage is to implement Invented Dialogs (Angelo & Cross, 1993). For this, you need to provide a variety of primary source quotes to seed the discussion. As your learners discuss the context of the challenge and their proposed solutions, they must weave into the dialog the provided quotes. Of course, the quotes must seamlessly fit into the conversation. The goal here is to make sure our learners reflect on the context of the challenge to ensure their intended solutions, at this juncture, are appropriate for the intended end-user.

The combination of these two strategies propels our learners into the consideration of new perspectives on the challenge and their so-far developed ideas for a solution. They very well may find they need to hop back into Stage Two to tweak their ideas or conduct additional research and engage in more inquiry. That's perfectly acceptable and encouraged, as needed.

Days Two and Three of Stage Three

Stage Three is the perfect time to introduce fiction as a case study related to the challenge. If you aren't an ELA teacher, again, there is no need to worry about themes, plots, and settings. Instead, use the characters in the story to develop an empathetic understanding for a similar challenge, as I noted earlier in this chapter. The use of a fictional character is a non-threatening way to introduce a different perspective before moving on to the perspectives from our technical experts. However, if you aren't sold on the idea of a fiction text, a case study from a historical example serves a very similar purpose. Keep in mind that this case study does not need to be from a hundred or more years ago. A worthy news story from a few months or even a few days before holds just as much weight. In fact, the more recent the story, the more likely your learners are to connect to its relevance.

Day Four of Stage Three

If you haven't already partnered your learners with technical experts, now is the time to do so. Of course, the earlier you can bring in technical experts, the better off you are in the long run. However, if you are short on connections with technical experts or if your technical experts don't have unlimited time to connect with your learners, it is fine to wait until this stage.

As your learners connect with these experts, you may find your expertise is needed, as well. As the educational expert, you might want to encourage the exchange between your learners and the experts as a protocol to frame the work that they do together. Otherwise, depending on the expert, there may be a lot of downtime if they are unused to working with preteens and very young teenagers. Thus, the Reversal Technique is perfect for this stage, as our technical experts help our learners to reverse the problem to generate new insight into it. I also encourage you to ask your technical experts to bring a reading for your learners to investigate that challenges their perspective on the project. While this is a bit tricky in terms of an appropriate level of reading, most technical experts can walk your learners through some of the finer points of the text. This reading does, however, serve to strengthen the academic vocabulary we have introduced through the challenge.

I would be remiss if I didn't mention the need for your technical experts to offer their feedback during this part of the project process. While not formally steeped in literacy, your learners should incorporate the expert feedback into a formal written reflection. This written reflection must include any tweaks and changes they will make from this feedback. Thus, again, our learners may find themselves looping back into Stage Two for a short period of time.

Literacy in Stage Four of Project Assessment

> **Actions and Consequences**
>
> How do we know if our learners have considered the potential positive and negative impacts of their proposed solution?
>
> 2–3 days

Day One of Stage Four

As our learners move into the consideration of the positive and negative possibilities that may arise out of their proposed solutions, a Say Something protocol works well. For this, you must choose a text for all of your learners to consider. At selected portions of the text, ask your learners to stop and "say something" about what they have read. While I prefer to do this as a partner activity, it is possible to do it in smaller groups, or even in a large group discussion. Any way that you choose to do it, I encourage you to require your learners to first write their "something" about what they just read before they share it out. This provides you with that all-important formative assessment data point and ensures that everyone participates, even in a large group setting.

Day Two of Stage Four

Again, we have an option of protocols to introduce here. The Reframing Matrix allows our learners to look to the potential of their solution ideas as they consider the impact on people, products, planning, and potential. This can be completed in teams and shared out for additional feedback and final tweaking to the solution. However, you may want to use another protocol such as the Pass Around Strategy in which your class of learners develop a story around a given prompt. This prompt can either be developed by you or developed by your learners. The more frequently they engage in this protocol, the more likely they will be to create their own prompts. In either case, the prompt should be developed as a scenario in the future in which the offered solution is put into place. Thus, our learners must consider the possible positive and negative outcomes of their solution. In fact, you can require them to write two stories to reflect on what they see as the positive and negative potential of their solution.

Day Three of Stage Four

Reflection now continues through the use of strategies that assist your learners to see additional impacts that their solution may have on their intended end-user. The use of SCAMPER (substitute, combine, adapt, modify, put to another use, eliminate, and reverse) teaches our learners to better view how their solution relates to any other tried solutions out there. In doing so, the hope is that they will modify as needed to better reflect a unique solution. More importantly, SCAMPER enhances our learners' understandings of what may happen as a result of their proposed solutions. Feel free to incorporate an additional text with this tool to aid in the broadening of their reflection.

Literacy in Stage Five of Project Assessment

> **Options and Opportunities**
>
> How do we know if our learners have developed an actionable solution for their end-users?
>
> 2–3 days

Days One and Two of Stage Five

It's time for our learners to complete a final product evaluation to ensure it meets the challenge purpose and the needs of its end-user. If your learners are preparing to present to a panel of authentic audience members, there is the option to role-play possible presentation scenarios with them (Laur & Ackers, 2017). This day is also a good time to record practice presentations. Teams can provide feedback to one another through embedded comments if you use an online platform such as Vimeo. Otherwise, comments via Google Slides may suffice, as do face-to-face feedback sessions.

If a presentation isn't a summative product, utilize this day to make any additional adjustments to written pieces. This day is also a good time to bring in upper-grade levels for support (Laur & Ackers, 2017). Here, you might consider an upper-level honors or AP class. Virtual connections between classes are easier than ever through Google Docs or any other collaborative writing tool. Many teachers have also found success with community writing groups who serve as technical experts. For your technical experts, they may want to join you in class to work one-on-one with learners or small groups of learners. If this isn't an option, a virtual exchange is a welcome alternative. These final feedback opportunities create the space to fine-tune their work before submitting it to their authentic audience.

Day Three of Stage Five

If you have decided that a panel presentation is appropriate, we have finally made it to that day! I can't stress enough that this presentation day is not a typical presentation of learning where guests walk around to "ooh" and "aah" over dioramas or tri-fold posters. This presentation is a formal proposal of the solution to the challenge and why our expert audience should buy into our solution. Your learners have anticipated this time from the start of the challenge and should be excited. However, nerves are common. Don't worry though; the more frequently your learners participate in a presentation of this magnitude, the easier and more natural it becomes.

Don't expect your technical experts to provide the actual grade for your learners. You are still the educational expert in the classroom and are responsible for this portion of the assessment. Although, once your learners complete the presentation, don't be surprised if they are excited to discuss the results of it. A whole class discussion is appropriate but do a silent, individual written reflection as well (Laur & Ackers, 2017). In this written reflection, have your learners return to the "Back to the Future" protocol that you included in Stage One. This protocol provides a context for their thinking. As an additional component, ask your learners to set a goal for their next project. What do they want to work on getting better at as a team member, as a problem-solver, or as a communicator? Once they have established their goal, ask them to also include how they intend to reach that goal as well as what you can do to help them achieve it. This goal setting puts the action in their hands as they continue to self-direct their learning story.

No matter what grade level or content area you teach, reading and writing are embedded within our curricular responsibilities. A good friend of mine, Ted Malefyt, who runs the Stream School on the west side of Michigan, once reminded me that even though his outdoor program is about becoming one with science, he couldn't do what he does without making reading and writing a focus. The concepts of citizenship, history, and the physical and natural world are enhanced by the reading and writing we ask our learners to undertake. In our art courses, more teachers are asking their artists to blog about their creative process and read detailed accounts of artistic movements. Our music students write through musical compositions that use notes instead of letters. Even in math, we have shifted to an environment where our learners must reason, rather than merely work through algorithms without a context, as they maintain journals that reflect on their solution processes. As we generate authentic and relevant reading and writing situations within our classes, our learners now have a purpose for reading and writing that subsequently sustains their interest in the authentic challenge.

Time to Reflect
1. What are the writing connections to your authentic challenge that you immediately envision?
2. What are the reading connections to your authentic challenge that you immediately envision?
3. How will these literacy additions strengthen your learners' abilities to develop a viable solution for their end-user?
Record Any Questions You Have Here

5

Formative Assessments for Success

> How do I utilize formative assessment to inform my instruction and support my learners authentically?

I distinctly recall many days when I spied the pile of exit tickets at the edge of my desk and could not muster the energy to review them. It was far too easy to brush them off the desk and into the garbage can. I can't even remember a time when I had one of my learners ask me if I had graded them, much less reviewed them to provide feedback for improvements. At that point in my teaching career, I'm not entirely sure that I even understood the purpose behind formative assessment. I can't recall a single time that I used those exit tickets to adjust my instruction. Since I was very good at preplanning my lessons for the entire unit, I certainly didn't want to have to go back and make changes!

Now that you've spent time planning the starting points of your authentic challenge, it's time to move from a 30,000-foot view to the ground level as you think more concretely about our Five Stages of Project Assessment. For this, you may already have a plethora of formative assessment strategies that you utilize regularly. Perhaps those exits tickets are one of them. If so, don't worry – there is no need to throw these ideas out. Principally, formative assessment is still employed to gather data about your learners, and the analysis of that evidence is used to inform any necessary changes to your instruction. You will, however, expand your repertoire of strategies, protocols, and activities to enhance each stage of assessment to ensure your learners are successful in the challenge, whether or not their solutions and ideas come to fruition.

How do I utilize formative assessment to inform my instruction and support my learners' authentically? In Chapter 2, you connected your standards to what is relevant for your learners to craft your authentic challenge. In Chapter 3, you explored how to ensure your learning ecosystem is authentically transformed through instructional technology as aligned to SAMR and the ISTE Standards for Students. Now, it is necessary to uncover how to evaluate, at each stage, how well your learners are mastering standards for both the content and skills that you embed within the authentic challenge.

Think about formative assessments as a never-ending party conversation (Graff & Birkenstein, 2012). In a situation such as this, you come late to the party and attempt to join in with a group of strangers that are engaged in a rather heated conversation. If you were to assess the party discussion, you could make observations about body language, listen to comments, question opinions shared, and entice further debate through targeted comments. You might also share out one or two of your ideas and banter back and forth with the guests. However, once you leave, the discussion continues without you. Now, your assessment of the conversation is over, and if you were to rejoin the debate at a later time, you would have to start your evaluation all over again. Primarily, this brief visualization provides us with a meaningful way to consider how we can fully embed formative assessments at each stage of the project. To ensure we don't miss part of the "conversation," we have to determine ways in which we can track our learners even when we aren't there to participate in their personal experience. Additionally, we must encourage our learners to fully participate in the challenge rather than contribute random thoughts here and there before "leaving." Ideally, we make adjustments as needed to make sure our learners don't check out of the challenge due to frustration or boredom. To guarantee our learners participate fully in the challenge, we must confirm that our learners do, in fact, at all stages of the project, understand all of the elements necessary for their success. Moreover, this focus on formative assessment ensures that no one learner is at any point left behind in a challenge.

The Stages of Project Assessment

Tim Kubik and I redesigned the Stages of Project Assessment for completion using a formative rather than summative approach. Even Stage Five requires a compilation of developmental reviews before our learners are prepared to present, in whatever chosen format, their final ideas to their authentic audience. Remember, these stages have, however, evolved from planning to assessment points. Part of the reason for this is because formative assessments are inherently a way for us to plan as the outcome of an assessment informs any shifts we may need to make in our instruction. The change may be necessary for one learner, a small group of learners, or your entire class. Therefore, I suggest you use as many formal and informal opportunities to conduct formative checks as time allows. These checks may be as simple as an observation or as complex as a Pinwheel Discussion (see Appendix 1). In either case, the data we gather is vital for our learners' success in an authentic learning experience.

No one magic formative assessment works for all learners and at all stages. The type of analysis you may choose to conduct will depend on the needs of your learners and your need to gather a specific data point. However, the one formative assessment that I find is the most revealing across all stages and with all learners is a simple journal. Whether you decide to implement this journal as an online or analog approach is up to you. The basic premise of the journal is that our learners, each day, write a response to the challenge. This response might be a few sentences or a few paragraphs as it depends on each learner and the goals for that day's class. This journal also serves to assist your learners in the development of the literacy skills that you explored in the last chapter. Now, I'll break down the process in more detail to provide you with a better understanding of the purpose and implementation of the practice.

When you launch your challenge with an engaging activity, exciting reading, thought-provoking video clip, or onsite fieldwork, the goal is to link the launch to the challenging question in such a way that immediately sparks inquiry. From that challenge problem, you have learned from your reading thus far, that your learners now create a list of inquiry questions. This inquiry list can be the first entry into the journal. With the inquiry list, ask your learners to write what they think about the challenge. This first entry provides you with a pre-assessment of their understanding and helps you to start to plan some of your lessons, as needed. From this point, have your learners respond to the challenge question daily. Again, the length isn't necessarily as important as the content. These entries provide us with a window into the thinking processes of our learners. As long as you manage to keep up with reading these entries, you can head off any misconceptions before they become too deeply rooted. Typically, I try to go no more than two days between reading the entries. If it is a particularly heavy day of information, I don't skip a quick read.

There is no need to grade these entries for grammar and syntax. However, I can't help myself to make corrections. Instead, scan with a critical eye toward the development of your learners' critical thinking. If entries don't seem to progress in moving toward a viable solution, it is time to intervene. Additionally, if the entries show no reflection of changes in thinking due to feedback, it is appropriate to schedule a one-on-one conversation.

At first, your learners may find this process to be tedious. Don't be surprised if you get a few complaints. "We already answered this yesterday" is a common statement. My response is always, "If you fully answered the question yesterday, it must mean you're ready to present your solution to your audience today." I've never had a learner tell me they were! Gradually, they come to appreciate the chance to reflect on their learning. At the conclusion of the challenge, these journals serve as a story of the learning process.

Once the challenge has ended, and before you move on to the next unit, have your learners add one final entry into their journals. Ask them to record one or two goals for their next PBL experience. The goal could be as simple as to work better as a teammate or as complex as becoming more attuned with the challenges in my community and how they align with our class content. Once they have decided on a goal, ask them to also include how they intend to achieve that goal, as well as how you can assist them in attaining that goal. This personalization makes the goal relevant for your learners, as well as holding them accountable for trying to achieve the goal. Keep in mind that it is difficult to meet a goal in the allotted time for one unit only. A goal may very well carry over for several units, as your learners work hard at mastering standards and essential skills.

Daily journaling is only one option for an effective formative assessment. While I do advocate for its consistent use, I suggest your other formative assessments are a mix of options that provide a variety of data points throughout each of our stages. While some protocols and strategies may be more appropriate at one stage versus another, there is no hard rule on what you should use and when. Instead, consider what information you are trying to gather, and how you intend to analyze that information.

As you examine Table 5.1, consider the listed possible formative assessments for each stage as they align to a variety of indicators of skill growth and content mastery. Contemplate how each of these may support the indicators and answer the question aligned to each stage. As we move into the next section of this chapter, I break down each stage with a narrative of how you might formatively assess your learners to ensure you can answer the questions aligned to each stage. Please keep in mind that this narrative is only one possible view for assessment. I have not included all of the possibilities listed in Table 5.1. Please use what works for your learners and you. As you implement multiple projects, change up your tactic. You may find you like certain activities, protocols, or discussions over others. That's part of the beauty of this pedagogical framework. There is no one right way to implement it! As you explore, try, and discover, also refer to Appendix 1 for additional ideas on formative assessment strategies

Table 5.1 Stages of Project Assessment Through a Formative Lens

Stages of Project Assessment	Indicators of Skill Growth and Content Mastery	Opportunities to Reflect on Needed Instructional Adjustments
Stage One: Challenge and Purpose How do we know if our learners understand and are invested in the challenge?	♦ Document their relevant connection to the project ♦ Articulate why the challenge is important to solve ♦ Identify the needs of their end-user	1. Space Method 2. GRASPS 3. Co-op Strip Paragraphs 4. Chalk Talks 5. Reframing Matrix 6. Problem Breakdown 7. 1,000 Word Pictures 8. Mind Map
Stage Two: Inquiry and Ideas How do we know if our learners have explored multiple pathways to a solution?	♦ Conduct research based on primary and secondary sources of information ♦ Data collection and analysis ♦ Develop several possible ideas to share with the group/peers	1. Mentimeter 2. Three-Step Interview 3. Open-Narrow-Close 4. Reversal Technique 5. Circle Square Triangle Reflection 6. Anchor Charts 7. Brain Drain 8. Text Clue Conclusion Groups
Stage Three: Context and Perspective How do we know if our learners have considered end-user needs and technical expert feedback?	♦ Discuss the implications of the given context of the challenge versus another possible context ♦ Receive and apply feedback provided by technical experts ♦ Forecast the impact of the solution for the end-user	1. Critical Dialogue 2. Say Something 3. Pass the Problem 4. Feedback Carousel 5. Café Conversations 6. Invented Dialogs 7. Notability 8. Three Misunderstandings
Stage Four: Actions and Consequences How do we know if our learners have considered the potential positive and negative impacts of their proposed solution?	♦ Compare and contrast the possible positive and negative outcomes of the solution ♦ Complete a cost–benefit analysis of their solution ♦ Provide a justification for any and all changes made	1. Think It Through 2. To Be or Not to Be 3. SCAMPER 4. Ranking Alternatives 5. Random Picture Story 6. Consequence and Sequel 7. Process Grid 8. Pinwheel Discussion
Stage Five: Options and Opportunities How do we know if our learners have developed an actionable solution for their end-users?	♦ Review the discarded ideas in favor of the given solution ♦ Anticipate how effective the proposed solution will be twenty years from now ♦ Predict how the challenge could extend into the future	1. Café Conversations 2. Reflective Central Idea Diagram 3. SWOT Analysis 4. Spider Web Discussion 5. Socratic Seminar 6. Snowball Discussion 7. Sound Bite 8. Yarn-Yarn

that may not be included in this table or in the narrative that follows. Please note that some of the reflection portions of this table were borrowed from Laur and Ackers (2017).

> **Stage One: Challenge and Purpose**
>
> How do we know if our learners understand and are invested in the challenge?

Stage One is all about ensuring our learners buy into the project while simultaneously certifying they have considered what they need to figure out to be successful in the challenge. This process can be challenging for us, as it is difficult to let go of control in the classroom. Remember, we don't necessarily know the pathway our learners might choose as they delve into this authentic learning experience. Since we can't necessarily predict with any accuracy what approach they might take, our formative assessment is vital from the very start of the project.

As we launch our PBL unit as an invitation to the learning, we offer our learners a chance to direct their learning journey. As such, the inquiry questions they pose from our launch help to guide us in providing the support our learners need from day one. This guide, of course, means our job in the classroom is even more critical than it was in a traditional sense. We have to be hyper-aware of what our learners need and can't assume they come to us with any predetermined knowledge. Even if we expect a particular grade level to teach specific concepts, this might not be the case. Since every learner comes to us with different backgrounds and experiences, the inquiry pathway for each learner may very well be different. This difference is part of what makes our authentic challenge a complex approach to education.

Let's pause for a moment and consider what questions our learners might ask as part of their inquiry list for a challenge. If we use an example from Appendix 3, we might have our learners ask any of the following questions to the problem, "How can we attract an affordable public transportation system that will meet the needs of our community for the next twenty-five years?"

- What is public transportation?
- What is considered to be affordable?
- What do our citizens want in a public transportation system?
- What has worked for other communities who have adopted a new public transportation system?

These questions might seem basic to some, but they are the most important formative assessment you will conduct in the course of your project implementation. While we might assume that everyone in our class knows about public transportation by the time they reach upper elementary school, if we have a learner or group of learners who have never taken public transportation (other than a school bus), they may not know the answer to this question. If we didn't ask for this inquiry list of questions, we might never know that some of our learners are unclear about public transportation. Effectively, one or more of our learners may have misread the purpose of the challenge from the start. Thus, this first vital formative assessment of the project paints a picture of some of the more traditional lessons you might incorporate at the beginning of your challenge.

These inquiry questions are what will eventually lead to more questions in Stage Two of our project assessment. But, for now, let's think about how to carry out this process of asking inquiry questions from the start of the project. As I noted earlier in this chapter, you might consider having your learners record their inquiry questions in their journals. However, this isn't a requirement. No matter how you intend to keep track of the inquiry questions, please make sure each learner creates their list to start the process. You might want to give them a required number of questions to pose when you first begin a PBL approach. However, the more familiar your learners are with this process, the less likely you will need to provide this type of guidance. Similarly, you can always start with question starters as probes into their thinking. I like the question dice from Kagan that lists prompts such as "how," "what," "would," "might," and others. When you roll the two die, the combination of word prompts assists learners in creating a question.

Once each learner records any questions they might have, now is the time to compare questions. Have learners partner up, initially, and then move into two pairs that form a group. Eventually, you want to share as a class to create a master list of questions. Keep in mind this list is a living document that will change. At any time, your learners need to feel like they can add questions they uncover during Stage Two. Once your learners assemble the master inquiry list, have them take the time to affinity map the questions. This affinity map requires them to create the categories into which they can place the questions and provide further guidance and direction for Stage Two. The affinity mapping process is also a formative assessment that directs any lessons that you may need to develop and implement to meet the needs of your learners as you ensure they understand the challenge and the purpose for it. Keep in mind that this means your days of preplanning entire units of lessons are all but over. While you may have an idea of some of those lessons, you must also be keenly aware that some of those lessons may never come to fruition and others will need to be designed from scratch based on the information you gather during this stage.

It is also a good idea to have your learners complete a SPACE Method document to figure out where each one is in their understanding of the process. Here, our learners summarize, process, analyze, connect, and evaluate. Additionally, a Problem Breakdown is necessary before moving on to Stage Two. With the Problem Breakdown, our learners have the opportunity to add any inquiry questions to their initial list. In this protocol, our learners list the steps they think that they must complete in order to solve the problem. Then, these steps are reframed as questions. If you have already done the initial inquiry list first as individuals, this activity is a good team approach for organizing thoughts and ideas before research commences in Stage Two.

> **Stage Two: Inquiry and Ideas**
>
> How do we know if our learners have explored multiple pathways to a solution?

Once our learners go through the affinity mapping process and have clearly articulated the purpose of the challenge as it relates to their end-users, we begin to map out lessons we might teach to scaffold their research. We also want to collect possible resources to support them as they gather information and collect data. Here, I encourage you to connect with your library media specialist for any assistance in compiling sources from your reference section, nonfiction collection, or even those literature books that might serve as the case studies we discussed in Chapter 4. This point in the project is also a time when he or she can conduct a lesson on how to use any online databases to which your district might subscribe.

It is helpful, at this point, if your learners have access to their Lexile, Dibels, or DRA score to assist them in choosing books that are appropriate for them. Remember our NetTrekker source, as well, to gauge a suitable reading level for a given website. Make a connection with your reading specialist or your ELL teacher to assist in finding alternative sources for those learners who need extra support.

If you have access, choose an online platform to which your learners can share their research with their teammates, if they are in groups or the whole class. Social booking with sites such as Diigo or Del.ic.ious enhances the collaborative aspect of the research. I start my learners with a set of tagged sites and ask them to add to the sites. As you review the sites that they add, you conduct an informal formative assessment of their understanding of the possible pathways to solve the challenge. If you decide to use Diigo in place of another social bookmarking site, your learners can also highlight and annotate their text for a more in-depth look at how well they are exploring the solution pathways and as a "talking to the text" approach to reading. Alternatively, you might use an Open-Narrow-Close protocol if you want to exclude digital tools.

It is important to note that all of your learners, rather than a select few, must conduct research. It is important to reiterate, if your learners are working in teams, do not split them into predefined roles such as "researcher" or only that assigned researcher learns how to research! Instead, breaking up the research into assigned segments ensures all of our learners increase their mastery of this skill, all while decreasing the amount of time it takes to research, as a whole. Individual research also gives us the ability to tailor any supports we may need to provide to any one learner or group of learners as we formatively assess reading, inference, research, and writing skills (Laur & Ackers, 2017).

As initial research from databases, reputable websites, and nonfiction texts filters through, discussions with our learners are valuable at this juncture of the project. These discussions might take place in small groups or with a whole class. Online discussions via a site such as Primary Pad allow you to manage and facilitate all discussions simultaneously, as you tab from discussion to discussion. The color-coding of each participant provides a quick visual assessment of who is participating and at what level. A deeper read of the conversations gives us a better insight into the critical thinking processes of our learners. Here, we can jump into a conversation and pose a question or prompt to guide our learners as and when needed.

A full class discussion may be a viable option, as well. Try using a Socratic Seminar or a Spider Web Discussion to determine what lesson scaffolds you may need to plan in the coming days. Both of these discussion types are described in more detail in Appendix 1, as I have my take on how to implement each of them. While these two discussions, listed in Table 5.1 above, are viable for Stage Five, I also reference them here as an alternate approach that allows your learners to collaboratively build meaning of the research and arrive at a definitive interpretation of it.

When our learners are ready to produce initial ideas for a solution, the Reversal Technique is an option for helping to scaffold this process. With this technique, our learners must determine ways in which they could cause the problem. The goal, here, is to generate reverse solution ideas that help to create a new pathway of looking at the challenge. Another option, however, might simply be to engage in a Brain Drain activity. This activity formalizes the brainstorming process to ensure all learners participate, as well as providing a scaffold for generating ideas. Here, you initiate the drain with prompts at the top of a 3×6 grid. Now, your learners, in small groups, use the prompts to fill in the empty spaces. These initial ideas give you a good idea of any misconceptions that may arise before your learners get too far into the development of their solution.

First ideas may not be viable ones, and that is entirely okay. Remember, we don't want to push our preconceived notions onto our learners' developments. I promise you that your learners will move away from non-viable ideas once they receive feedback. However, we also want our learners to recognize if their plans won't work. Therefore, we can use questioning techniques to probe deeper into their thinking so that any flaws may reveal themselves.

While I am not a huge fan of the use of "tinkering" as part of our educational lexicon these days, Stage Two does create a space for our learners to try out ideas. Our learners will make modifications to their ideas based on their research, collected data, and, eventually, feedback that is evident in Stage Three. If their first idea is their last idea in exact form, not enough inquiry has occurred, and we haven't completed adequate formative assessments. This form of tinkering, however, doesn't necessarily mean you want to schedule time in the makerspace for your learners. While, on occasion, this may be appropriate, often a makerspace session produces just another project rather than an authentic learning experience. Don't assume that crafting an artifact out of pipe cleaners and cardboard leads to the complex solution we desire our learners to develop.

As we review first ideas, we already have some formative data to use as we determine what additional supports we may need to provide our learners. Here, the written reflections of our challenge question journal entries give us a deeper look into each learner's thought process. If we want to find out why our learners made some decisions over others, we should conduct one-on-one and group meetings. Now, we have the opportunity to ask follow-up questions, which causes our learners to reflect in a more targeted way. These meetings also provide us with better formative assessment data compared to written reflections, as some of our learners may have a difficult time expanding on their written work or may simply choose not to write revealing information (Laur & Ackers, 2017).

Stage Two, in many cases, may be our longest stage, as our learners cycle back and forth between research, ideas, and revamped ideas from Stage Three. This inquiry progression is why formative assessment is so critical at this stage. Without our assessment, conceivably, we could get to the end of the project and have quite a few surprises from our learners. Instead, our formative assessments should allow us to predict our summative assessment at the conclusion of Stage Five.

> **Stage Three: Context and Perspective**
>
> How do we know if our learners have considered end-user needs and technical expert feedback?

An authentic challenge requires the consideration of the appropriate context for that challenge. Think of it this way, the sometimes excessive droughts that are often experienced by the state of California are very hard for someone in a south-eastern state such as South Carolina that does not have any desert land and is, by its very location, a very humid state. Therefore, if we asked our learners in South Carolina to come up with a solution to lessen the effects of a drought on California, their contextual understanding would be skewed. Therefore, we want to ensure we formatively assess our learners' understanding of the context of a challenge and the subsequent solution.

One of the ways in which you might decide to evaluate contextual understanding and application of the context is through a Pass the Problem activity. Here, you provide your learners with several different case studies (or, if you're doing this for the first time, you may want to stick with only one or two case studies) of a similar problem to the one your learners must solve. Each group starts by listing the first step that they perceive to be the way in which they should solve the question. The groups then pass the problem to the next group who will attempt to list what they believe is the second step in addressing the case study. The passing continues until all groups think the listed steps have been exhausted. Keep in mind that one group may determine that a previous group or groups missed a step and can insert their thinking in the middle of the offered steps. If you are so inclined, and depending on the culture of your classroom, you might decide to conduct this between individuals in a team rather than in a classroom full of teams. In either case, this activity helps teams and individuals to consider the context of solving a challenge.

Similarly, a Café Conversation can assist your learners in delving into the context of a challenge. In this activity, instead of systematically deciding the steps that have to happen to solve a problem, a discussion leader is situated at a table with chart paper and a question stem or case study related to the context of the challenge. For instance, you ask how the problem would change in twenty years, or how the problem would affect a community similar to yours but located in a different part of the country. The team leader stays at the table, and small groups of learners rotate to each table for a predetermined amount of time. These learners jot down ideas and answers to the question stems or about the case study. As each group rotates, they share additional views, thus, deepening the context of the challenge. Finally, the team leaders share out the information once all teams have had the opportunity to add to the conversation.

Once our learners have a firm grasp on the context of the challenge, it is equally important to provide opportunities for our learners to interact with technical experts. Technical experts bring a fresh perspective to our learners' ideas. With real-world experience in the field in question, these experts ask key questions that we may not be prepared to ask. Thus, they extend our learners' capacity to reflect on their ideas that have yet to be fully formulated. They also provide valuable feedback that creates a capacity to question oneself as a learner and problem solver (Laur & Ackers, 2017).

Since it is highly unlikely that a technical expert can spend the entire project with your learners, you will have to explore other options for your learners to share their learning journey with the experts. One possibility is to use the online tool, Notability, to record the ideas of your learners as they move through Stage One and, most importantly, Stage Two. With this tool, your learners can pool written notes, photos, and sketches into one document as a visual progression of their thinking. This document helps to tell the progressive story of how your learners have, individually or in groups, arrived at a possible solution for review by the technical experts.

We, the teacher, and peers from the class cannot compete with the value that the feedback from our experts adds. With each nugget of honesty provided or question prompted, our learners shift their perspective on the challenge. This processed feedback might mean your learners need to return to Stage Two, or in some extreme cases Stage One. Additionally, the feedback from our technical experts can assist us in planning additional supports when and if needed to clarify any contextual questions or decisions about the offered solution's viability.

> **Stage Four: Actions and Consequences**
>
> How do we know if our learners have considered the potential positive and negative impacts of their proposed solution?

No matter what ideas emerge from combined Stages Two and Three, those ideas have consequences attached to them. Any action taken on a proposed plan has the potential to effect change in either a positive or negative manner. Thus, it is essential for our learners to consider a cost–benefit analysis of their ideas in Stage Four.

One of your options for an early formative assessment in this stage is to complete a ranking alternatives activity. In this rather easy task, have the sum of your groups list their ideas for the whole class. As a class, rank the solutions for their feasibility and the ones that are least likely to have a negative impact on the challenge. From these rankings, you have the makings of any discussion protocol. A Spider Web Discussion or Socratic Seminar feeds out of the ranking alternatives activity. Alternatively, you could have teams informally debate with each other on the value of the ideas. Just as tellingly, a Five Whys protocol that takes place with partners sheds light on future implications. In this protocol, each partner takes a turn asking five why questions based on the answers provided. The deeper into the protocol our learners get, the more difficult it is to ask a "why" question and the more difficult it is to answer the question.

A diverse way of getting to the heart of what your learners are thinking in this stage is to implement a Random Pictures Story. For this activity, you need to plan several days ahead to collect random pictures that your learners will use to tell their story. I suggest checking with your library media specialist for old magazines that you could cut up. I tend to like the science magazines, as they have some of the best pictures without an ad plastered in the middle of them.

Once you have cut out your pictures, give groups of students a set of pictures. If you have a larger group, six pictures are generally enough with one given to each learner. If you have smaller groups, give each learner two pictures to allow for the creation of a complex story. It is essential to have enough pictures to ensure that a well-developed story can emerge. The rest of the work is up to your learners. Now, they use the images to tell two separate accounts. One story gives the positive outcomes that result from their proposed solutions, and the other story explores the negative possibilities. Using the same set of pictures in this case also encourages critical thinking and higher levels of communication that I examine in Chapter 7.

It is important that we invite our learners to think about the consequences of their actions. Our learners are still maturing and often act quickly without regard to the implications that come with their efforts. A stop and pause mentality is useful for everyone, as with reflection comes growth as a learner.

Stage Five: Options and Opportunities

How do we know if our learners have developed an actionable solution for their end-users?

School has traditionally been about knowing the right answer or the design of a presentation that looked like it was crafted by a professional, rather than a focus on a learner's ability to find potential solutions to given challenges (Laur

& Ackers, 2017). As your learners move away from that one right answer attitude and toward a desire to meet the needs of their end-user, we must ensure they have considered all of the possibilities and then articulate the justification of why they settled on the proposed solution. Ultimately, what might work as a solution in one context may not work in another, and the explanation of this is just as important as the solution itself. Moreover, it is vital for our learners to further explain how the solution might affect the future of the challenge. Our learners should also communicate the opportunities for further development as time goes on and possible new technologies emerge.

This is a great place for us to implement a SWOT analysis for our learners to review all of their work. What are the strengths, weaknesses, opportunities, and threats their final solution might face when reviewed by experts? (Laur & Ackers, 2017). This document is useful for your learners as a final check on any tweaks they may want to make to their solutions, as well as an important record for them to share with their authentic audience as they discuss why they chose a particular option despite any potential negative consequences.

Before any final formal presentation or submission of work to an authentic audience, our learners should have the occasion to engage in a formalized discussion about their solutions and what open-ended opportunities still exist in the challenge, even with the implementation of the proposed ideas. There are several ways in which you might choose to do this. I've mentioned the Spider Web and Socratic Seminar possibilities already. You might also want to try the Yarn-Yarn discussion as a way to provide visual cues to your learners on who has participated. As your learners wrap a piece of yarn around their fingers and pass the yarn ball to the next speaker, patterns emerge on who talks the most frequently and who might be better at listening.

The creation of a sound bite is one of the ultimate ways in which your learners can showcase the innovativeness of their answer to the challenge. The sound bite format requires them to use targeted language to convince their audience as to why their solution is the most viable one for the end-user. In an elevator pitch type of presentation, learners must condense their presentation information into twenty-seven words within nine seconds that reveal three overall thoughts. The sound bite is a targeted way for you to review any final feedback opportunities. Of course, any formalized presentation will need further development, but this pitch serves as a way to focus your learners on the most important points of their presentation. Your learners can also use it as an introductory attention-grabber before beginning.

Through the completion of multiple formative assessment strategies in each of the Five Stages of Project Assessment, our learners have effectively produced a portfolio of their growth and mastery of the content and standards

(Laur & Ackers, 2017). This window into their project journey, at each stage, affords us the privilege to meet the needs of every learner rather than the presumed needs of the entire class. While taking this planning tactic for an authentic challenge leaves much undetermined on a daily basis, it subsequently provides the opportunity to tailor our instruction such that it also mirrors the real world in the responsiveness to our learners.

Time to Reflect

1. How have your ideas about formative assessment evolved from reading this chapter?

2. What is one formative assessment tool that you have used previously that you will now use differently to support you in your quest to gather data about your learners during the authentic challenge you implement?

3. What is one new formative assessment tool that you will try with your learners immediately, and how will that tool help you to gather the necessary data needed to inform your instruction?

Record Any Questions You Have Here

6

Levels of Complexity

> How do I create a classroom ecosystem that allows complexity to emerge through an authentic project?

I have a confession to make: I must have a Netflix series on hand to watch at all times. I watch my shows as I make dinner and fold the laundry. It is my guilty pleasure. As I finish one series and search for another, I often start a show only to have my interest quickly wane by the second or third episode. Sometimes, my interest is shot before the first 10 minutes have passed in episode one. As I've tried to analyze my viewing habits, I've decided it boils down to the complexity of the show. If there aren't enough of layers for me to uncover, I get bored.

Recently, I finished watching the entire seven seasons of *Scandal*. (I promise it took me weeks, as binge-watching over a long weekend isn't my thing.) One episode, in particular, really stood out. In season two, episode seven, Huck, one of the main characters, was asked a "what would you do" question. He responded, "Hypotheticals are pointless. Come back to me when you have a real-life situation." That quote spoke volumes as I easily related it to our classrooms full of preteens and young teens that desperately want to engage in real life.

Before you read any further, contemplate your answers to the following questions:

- How much of the real world do you bring into your classroom?
- How does your content connect to the real world?
- In what ways have you connected your learners to real-world, technical experts?
- How frequently do your learners ask you, "Why do I need to know this?"

I am fairly certain the generalized responses to these questions probably relate to simulated experiences that attempt to mirror the real world. It isn't uncommon to start on the journey of PBL with pretend classroom activities. Often, PBL literature talks about authenticity as a spectrum. On the one side, very controlled simulations that reflect what professionals do in the real world are considered to fall into this category. For instance, a fifth-grade class of learners who have to solve a medical mystery and present their findings to the class and invited adults is a simulated experience. While this may pique the interest of some budding young medical professionals, it is, at its core, a simulation.

On the other side of the spectrum, we have work that happens in the real world translate into the authentic challenges we invite our learners to participate in solving. This book has been peppered with quite a few ideas as examples. However, we have yet to break down the complexity of authentic learning experiences. While I find value in the work on the far left of the spectrum as scaffolds to a deeper challenge, I also argue that these simulated experiences, as stand-alone efforts, do not get to the heart of complex thinking and learning.

How do I create a classroom ecosystem that allows complexity to emerge through an authentic project? Before we can answer this question, we need to understand the difference between the levels of complexity and that which is complicated. To illustrate the distinctions between the two, let's for a moment turn to basketball or, if you prefer, substitute this example with hockey or almost any other team sport.

Any good coach establishes a series of plays for their team. These scripted events, during practice, can be complicated for some players to master. At first, the position on the court and the sequence of events confuse and confound some guards and forwards, until they've run the plays so many times that they become second nature. However, when game time comes, the complexity of the plays emerge. When the coach calls for the play, the players must now contend with the added pressure of guarding the opposing team and passing without a steal. Of course, the shot, itself, is a complex evolution impacted by when the shooter is clear to release the ball, based on the angle, velocity, and potential interference by an opposing player. We can also add in the layer of complexity if our star shooter, for whom the coach designed the play, is sitting on the bench due to an injury.

Now that we have a basic understanding of the difference between complicated and complex in a non-classroom context, let's dig into the difference that we see in the classroom. Tiny house projects are all the rage in some math classes I visit. Area and perimeter are the staple geometric concepts for this project design, and it applies to a variety of grade levels that range from third to seventh. You can even Google "tiny house project," and the result is a plethora of sites including ones that describe their contents as a "PBL activity." (The use of the word "activity" is our first sign that we have a complicated task rather than a complex challenge.) If you were to have your learners follow the step-by-step instructions on how to craft a three-dimensional model of a tiny house, you have the start of complication. If a learner misses one step, they can't go on to the next. In fact, the first step in the project I found is to "Read ALL directions in Tiny House Parts." Moreover, these provided steps come from the teacher rather than the learners determining what they need to complete for a successful design process. The final product, graded by the teacher, has a variety of options for what it looks like based on each learner's design. In a final analysis of this project, overall, there is little room for deviation and learner inquiry throughout its execution.

If we take the same tiny house concept, we can easily shift it to a complex challenge. Of course, the first thing we want to do is eliminate the step-by-step process introduced in the complicated approach. While it is perfectly acceptable to have requirements for a project, these defined phases in our Googled example are limiting. Instead, we can introduce inquiry by allowing our learners to investigate any building requirements for the tiny houses, which are dependent on a community. In some cases, a tiny house development plan may not currently be allowed in your locale. Therefore, an additional layer of complexity is to add working with a planning commission on adopting regulations to permit tiny houses. Furthermore, if your learners had a client for the tiny house that had particular wants, we again introduce complexity. Finally, the geographic location of the tiny house also presents a complex situation. The lot for the placement of the tiny house requires a variety of considerations from our learners, as well. Depending on your grade level, the areas of complexity that you address shift. Additionally, you may choose to integrate different content areas within this challenge, as social studies and ELA are possible avenues for expansion with additional standards and content.

Hopefully, you are beginning to understand the difference between complicated assignments and complex challenges. Although, there are plenty of instances when complicated in the classroom is sometimes confused with rigor. Rigor, as typically defined in the schools where I have taught, relates to the practice of higher-order thinking for learners to deepen their understanding of content. Often and especially in higher tracked classes in upper elementary and honors classes in middle school, rigor equates to more work. The argument for more work, in later elementary, is often attributed to the need for middle school preparation, with a similar sentiment in middle school to prepare learners for high school. This work is often synonymous with drudgery and chores. Thus, it is necessary to shift this mindset from one in which work only pays off in grades and promotion to the next level. This shift must be to one that empowers our learners to push forward due to the dividends of empowerment as a learner. To empower our learners, we must stop and figure out what motivations are needed to move them to those higher levels of thinking rather than solely completing complicated work.

All too frequently, our learners focus on a grade as the result of their learning. The means to this end is the completion of whatever task, assignment, or test they must pass to make the grade. Unfortunately, for some learners, the grade isn't enough motivation to get them to participate fully in whatever we ask them to complete. For a few learners, the tasks are too easy, and the lack of challenge causes them to act out. For other learners, the activities are too complicated and result in a complete shutdown that ranges from skipping class to skipping school entirely. Of course, we can't forget our learners that fall somewhere in between the two ends of this spectrum.

To illustrate, let's consider my fifth-grade daughter. Recently, she came home in tears for what she referred to as "failing her math test." In reality, it was an 89 percent, but she's a perfectionist. As I reviewed the test, I realized she had, in fact, not missed a single question based on the wording of the problems. However, she had listed the equation that she used to solve the problem rather than the expression that was requested in the point value explanation. I know, it is semantics, but semantics created a rather dire evening of crying and a newfound "hate" of math. And, while I rarely interfere with what goes on in the classrooms of my own children, I couldn't help but write a note on the test I had to sign: "The equations are a more complex way of thinking about the problems than the expression, as she solved for an unknown variable." Complicated can lead to tears from our learners who fall somewhere in between those at either end of the spectrum who shut down. While we may not always witness these tears in the classroom, they can be a very real phenomenon behind closed doors. As an educator and a parent, I want to see tears of joy rather than tears of frustration.

While I know grades are a necessary evil, and I don't anticipate a widespread demise of their implementation anytime soon, the complexity of authentic learning can change the grading narrative. If we move away from a checklist of task requirements and toward an open-ended, multiple pathways learning process, grades become an afterthought for our learners. Instead of focusing on a good grade or figuring out ways to beat the system to avoid a bad grade, our learners now embrace the challenge not as a means to an end but as a need for their audience of end-users. As you review Table 6.1, note how the complicated activities in the left-hand column have listed two of the many steps that must happen in order for the task to be completed successfully. For these activities, generally speaking, the efforts in one context will mirror those in another. In contrast, on the right-hand side of the column, our complex learning experiences require our learners to peel back the layers of what they must accomplish in order to solve the challenge.

The Complex Systems of Authentic Learning

There is a duality of complexity embedded within an authentic learning experience. First and foremost, we intrigue our learners with the challenge because the

Table 6.1 Moving from Complicated Activities to Complex Experiences

Complicated Project Activity	**Complex Learning Experience**
Picking up litter for a community service project: ♦ Find volunteers ♦ Disposal of trash	Design a product that is biodegradable that won't add to the litter problem
Follow a multi-step recipe ♦ All listed ingredients and amounts provided ♦ Mixing procedures and baking temperatures given	Craft a casserole, from scratch, using only the ingredients that are on hand
Find the most efficient route from Point A to Point B ♦ Follow the road possibilities ♦ Calculate the given distances	Design an updated evacuation route in case of a major emergency
Paint a picture using a model provided ♦ Use the indicated colors ♦ Place objects in designated spots	Paint a picture with only a blank canvas, paints, and imagination
Showcase a musical from a list of approved options ♦ Cast must learn lines/songs ♦ Costumes and set design are crafted from suggested templates	Score a new musical that features a strong storyline

solution is for an end-user. They want to explore and delve into the challenge because their ideas for a solution have the potential to effect change. This solution requires the need for our learners to consider for whom they are solving the problem and in what context their end-users desire a solution. Thus, a challenge in one environment for one set of users may require a separate solution in another location for another audience. While our end-users are a fundamental layer of complexity, as is the situational context of the challenge, the complexity also emerges from the open-endedness of the challenge.

As reviewed in Chapter 2, it isn't enough to bring our learners to the levels of application and evaluation in Bloom's. If we stop here, our learners mire down in complicated work. Sometimes, the complicated work we assign is actually stuck at the understanding level of Bloom's. Thus, when written at the creation level of Bloom's, our authentic challenges open up possibilities for complexity to emerge in the challenge. See Table 6.2 for examples of assignments that do not reach the creation level of Bloom's.

As you study Table 6.2, consider each example and how you might extend them from complicated to complex undertakings. For instance, while we might make the argument that writing flashcards will help with the memorization of vocabulary words, if our learners fail to engage in a more complex application of the words, only those learners who are good at memorization will ever succeed.

Table 6.2 Complicated versus Complex

Complicated Activity	Bloom's Level	Why Complicated?
Complete 25 math problems at the conclusion of a lesson	Understanding/Application	♦ Not every learner needs to complete all 25 to show they have grasped this concept ♦ For those learners who struggle with the concept, the 25 problems lead to frustration
Read a chapter, define vocabulary words, and answer the questions at the end of each section	Remembering – vocab Understanding/Analysis/Evaluation – questions	♦ There is no interaction with the text when reading ♦ While some questions may be higher-level, often the answers are found directly in the text
Write flash cards for vocabulary words	Remembering	♦ Memorization is required to learn the words ♦ Tedious repetition is required
Write a book report	Understanding/Analysis/Evaluation	♦ Some book reports only ask for key details or interesting facts ♦ Most book reports require an opinion of the reader

Furthermore, after the vocabulary words show up on a test, the chances are pretty good that those words become a distant memory. Therefore, to add complexity to the task, our learners must use the words in the appropriate context as they explain a solution to a challenge and do so for an authentic audience. Now, the words become rooted in the memory of our learners and are far less likely to fade from their vernacular, and a complicated activity is used instead to scaffold for a much deeper experience.

Of course, it is easier to think about a lower-level Bloom's task as a complicated one. If we examine the book report example from Table 6.2, we can also envision how to push into more profound complexity. While sometimes a book report only requires a simple summary and list of essential or interesting facts, the higher cognitive premise of a report is to develop an overview of the book with character analysis and theme exploration. This development moves our learners higher up the ladder of Bloom's into the analysis and evaluation levels. However, this is where it stops. In this basic book report concept, what our learners do is report out discovered insight about the book they read. This insight may move into whether or not the book is recommended for others to read. In some instances, there might even be the option to extend the thinking into application with the conception of a book trailer via iMovie or Movie Maker. Be aware, however, that a book trailer is not at the creation level of Bloom's, as the trailer is purely a creative way to share information that is lower-level Bloom's.

A book report could turn into a case study for a much deeper authentic challenge. In this case, the character analysis becomes a foundational component as a perspective on how the challenge might resolve based on a proposed solution. As a different avenue to open up into complexity, your learners could write their own book. Of course, the book type is dependent on the context of your unit. From an ELA perspective, the book could be an anthology of short stories, poems, or even a compilation of children's stories. If you teach social studies, the collection of first-hand interviews turned into first-person narratives could relate to a variety of units. A group of student art pieces with accompanying creation of the story behind the art promotes a cross-curricular approach to complexity. In any of these instances, our learners challenge themselves to uncover new understandings, which are applied in new contexts.

Planning for Complexity

Many teachers, as they start to explore authentic project design, feel more comfortable when they plan out the entire project from start to finish based on exactly how their learners will develop their answer. This is because they can rely on their known resources and previous experiences and limit the surprise factor that often accompanies an open-ended learning experience. However, we must question the complexity of this approach as planning in detail removes opportunities for complex thinking. The unpredictability and dynamic relationship between interconnected parts of a complex challenge are removed when step-by-step planning occurs. Alternatively, many teachers who I encounter in my workshops or online coaching and classes, often request access to a fully developed project example. However, I always hesitate to immediately provide one, as it takes away some of the inquiry process in their personal project; that being to develop an authentic, relevant, and complex challenge for their learners.

Regularly, teachers unknowingly get into the habit of crafting an authentic challenge with little complexity. Heck, as I started writing this book, for several of the chapters, I boxed myself into a complicated situation. For the chapters I revised that were original to the PreK-3 book I've previously mentioned, I found the task terribly tedious and even laborious at times. I had to color-code the few words, sentences, and charts I wanted to keep, while I tried to rewrite but maintain the structural integrity of the rest of those chapters. For the completely new chapters such as this one that I wrote from scratch, I had a much easier time allowing the words to flow with no directed outline to guide me. Similarly, we can innocently craft a complicated project without intending to do so, and much of this complication comes when we attempt to script out too many lessons and ideas.

It is okay to want to plan out as much as possible for an authentic challenge. However, due to the complex nature of how a challenge may play out, it is nearly impossible to entirely plan for one. Thus, if you are starting on this journey, feel free to plan for some but not all of the challenge. The planning part will help you to feel more confident to implement the project with your learners, while allowing room for the project to morph into those unknown pathways that may very well emerge. Be prepared, however, to abandon any plans you may have created as dictated by the formative assessments you conduct and the divergent routes that spontaneously emerge at any given point in the process.

As you have explored this book, you have simultaneously been planning your own project for classroom implementation. Hopefully, by now, you have some sort of an outline of your project. Upon completion of your reading, you want to have a 30,000-foot view of your idea. What we don't want, however, is a scripted play-by-play experience for your learners, lest we end up with our tiny house example from the start of this chapter.

Complexity changes from project to project. Indeed, complexity changes within a project depending on the learners involved in the project. So, for all of you who are concerned that you may plan a project only to have to go back to the drawing board the next year and start from scratch, this isn't necessarily the case. It is conceivable that you may plan a project, implement the project, and decide it went so well that you want to implement it again. You may only need to make a few tweaks and changes from year to year, if your challenge is as open-ended as possible. As an illustration, think about your smartphone. A smartphone's design is updated on a yearly, if not biannual basis. The challenge, however, remains the same. How can we design a smartphone to meet the needs of our users? Of course, the needs of our users change, and the available technology for design changes rapidly. Thus, the designs alter to include stronger and lighter materials, longer battery life, improved security features, better photo elements, and probably quite a few features that we don't even know we need or want. Of course, we can't forget about how smartphones led to smart watches and smart speakers. This is complex design at its finest.

Once you are comfortable enough with project design as you ascertain the inclusion of specific content and standards, you may be ready to move into a co-design approach. When you ask for the support from a technical expert, complexity is nearly always an automatic presence in the challenge. This challenge is likely a real issue for the community partner. For instance, your partner may struggle with a redesign of playground equipment at the local park. This complex challenge is ripe for a social studies, math, or physical education class to evaluate, as they design a potential solution for the challenge.

We want to develop and cultivate these long-term, community partnerships as frequently as possible. Using community resources is often a complicated endeavor, while creating community partnerships builds a complex ecosystem built on mutual respect. These partnerships foster long-term growth and learning compared to an annual field trip. While there is nothing wrong with taking a field trip to a local site, think about how you could use that field trip to launch an authentic challenge, as you work with technical experts to explore the complex problems they encounter daily.

Ultimately, some of the most complex challenges materialize from your learners' desires to address problems that are relevant to them. In this situation, it requires you to let go of any preplanned efforts you may have developed. Moreover, you must be flexible to move around units if needed. Often, these challenges develop out of questions your learners pose. For instance, in *Authentic Learning Experiences: A Real-World Approach to Project-Based Learning*, I wrote about Erin McMahon's fifth-grade learner, in Frederick,

Maryland, who posed a question after a heavy rainstorm that turned into a challenge to create a rain garden. The question was simply, "What's all this yucky stuff?" Erin's ability to recognize the complexity that could emerge from this question was phenomenal, and the ultimate challenge they co-created was, "How can we help to eliminate the pollutants seeping into our schoolyard?" With this co-creation, we also move beyond engagement and into empowerment.

Often teachers hear the word engagement and assume the need to entertain throughout the challenge (Laur & Ackers, 2017). However, entertainment in a complex challenge is not our goal. Summarily, engagement can equate to an intriguing video, an opportunity to be actively up and moving, or participating in an interactive simulation. All of these examples are plausible scaffolds for a more complex challenge that leads to empowerment through the occasion to solve a meaningful problem. However, we do not want to stop at engagement. As such, an authentic challenge that provides for a variety of pathway possibilities presents our learners with a significant outlet for ownership. Some organizations call this "voice and choice."

"Voice and choice" is not a phrase I generally like to use. This phrase is far too limiting in its application, as it can be wrongfully inferred to allow learners to choose a topic to investigate that interests them. From this general exploration, I frequently see frustrated teachers who feel the learning gets lost in the process. Moreover, by simply allowing our learners to choose a passion for exploring, many standards may be difficult to apply to the project. Instead, I prefer to use personal alternatives.

Personal alternatives individualize the course your learners determine in an open-ended challenge. There is no one right or wrong way to solve the problem. As such, the complex possibilities are endless, and our learners are empowered to explore them. This open exploration leads to a narrowing down of the challenge question so that the personal alternative is apparent. Take a look at Table 6.3 for examples that illustrate a pathway that learners may choose to take in the challenges from Table 1.4 in Chapter 1. Keep in mind, this is only one alternative out of many possibilities, and depending on your grade level or content area, these may shift.

As we consider the possibilities for personal alternatives to the challenge, this is the perfect time to realize complexity can be differentiated. Our learners who are labeled as gifted, those who require learning support, or our English Language Learners (ELLs) now have the space to enter a challenge at a suitable level of complexity. Now, our gifted learners won't max out in the possibilities for enhancement, and our learners who

Table 6.3 Personal Alternatives

Challenge Launch	Personal Alternative
How can we craft a plan to make the future of aviation safer?	How can I design an alternative to boarding or exiting the plane?
How can we redevelop a use for the abandoned properties in our town?	How can I attract a new business to a vacant building?
How can we design a plan for the conservation of farmland?	How can I use alternative farming methods to conserve farmland?
How can we redesign the traffic patterns for a pedestrian and auto-heavy intersection?	How can I make crossing the street safer for school-aged children?
How can we convince the state government to increase the funding for our local library?	How can I increase resident usage of our local library to show that funding is necessary?

need additional help won't experience frustration from a challenge that is too overwhelming for them.

No matter what the current academic level of your learners, the use of an authentic learning experience provides them with the creative freedom to develop personal ideas to solve the challenge. Since there is no one right answer to the problem, and the inquiry process is the foundation of the instructional strategy, all learners have the opportunity to flourish in this environment. With an open-ended question, differentiation is automatically built-in to the inquiry process. Our learners who need additional support can complete the same project as our learners who need a push toward more challenging engagement. Thus, we have the occasion to provide diverse materials to meet each learner's needs. Moreover, we develop a class culture that doesn't cater to the whole but, instead, caters to small groups or individuals on an as-needed basis.

For our ELLs, through Bloom's creation level, the inquiry process provides a broader foundation to support the acquisition and mastery of language. The challenge makes vocabulary come to life and gives an innate purpose for reading a text. An authentic challenge promotes oral language proficiency through repeated collaborative conversations (Laur & Ackers, 2017). Of course, many of our GLAD (Guided Language Acquisition Design) strategies are appropriate as scaffolds to support these collaborative conversations; you can find several of these strategies listed in Appendix 1.

For our learners with an IEP or 504 Plan who may struggle to memorize information and take tests that box in their learning, the authentic challenge presents them with the space to think outside of the box. Rather than feel inadequate as a test taker, often these learners flourish as they have the newfound freedom to share their knowledge and understanding in an entirely new way. Frequently, these learners have higher creative capacities than our straight-A students who have aced the game of school. That's not to say that we won't have to provide these learners with the appropriate scaffolds when needed. While we may need to adapt readings or provide extra help with interpreting resources, these modifications only strengthen the outcomes our learners produce.

Our gifted learners frequently complain of boredom in the traditional classroom, and gifted pullout classes often only meet once or twice a week/cycle. As we introduce our gifted learners to an authentic challenge, the cognitive demands required of them increase tremendously. Since this newfound complexity may be a shock to some of our gifted learners, who typically complete assigned classroom activities with ease, we cannot forget to scaffold and support them just as we would for our ELLs and IEP learners. As they engage in the inquiry process, we can prod them to dig deeper into more complex research, which, in turn, leads them to more complex questions, and ultimately, more complex solutions.

Complexity and the Stages of Project Assessment

Now that we have a grasp on the complexity of authentic learning experiences and examples that distinguish between complicated and complex, let's consider how complexity unfolds in each stage of project assessment.

> **Stage One: Challenge and Purpose**
>
> How do we know if our learners understand and are invested in the challenge?

The complexity of a challenge instantly materializes when we write it at the creation level of Bloom's. When we have an open-ended question that has no one right answer, this provides the immediate prospect to link the issue to any relevant and meaningful connection to personal experiences. This link is the first layer of complexity. When our learners couple their individual familiarities into an analysis of the challenge, as a whole, they instantaneously see new pathways they would not have on their own. From here, we initiate the process of inquiry as our learners generate questions, think about how they might answer those questions based on personal experiences, and consider the guiding questions we ask that help them make connections between the two, as they ponder the unknown.

The unknown can be a scary endeavor for our learners to embark upon no matter what grade level or content area is addressed. The unknown necessitates a launch to the challenge so that it grabs the attention of our learners and gets them excited about the purpose of it. This launch could include any number of approaches that incorporate a visit to the site in question or a data set of information that directly confronts our learners with the need to solve the problem. The launch must also add another dimension of complexity for our learners, as they unpack the purpose of the challenge and for whom they must solve it. These end-users create a specific purpose based on time, location, and available resources. Each of these three contextual components elicits a complex way of viewing the challenge.

> **Stage Two: Inquiry and Ideas**
>
> How do we know if our learners have explored multiple pathways to a solution?

Inquiry is inherently a complex process when our learners are the ones asking the questions. In a traditional classroom, the opposite is true. Therefore, it can primarily seem complicated to our learners to initiate questions that arise out of the challenge. However, the questions are what lead our learners down any given pathway as they seek possible solutions to the problem. While it is necessary for us to monitor the inquiry process and prompt our learners' thinking through coaching, guidance, and facilitation, ultimately, we want the questions to be their own. These generated questions are the answers our learners seek to uncover as they propose potential solutions for their end-users.

The variety of ideas our learners explore, and the one upon which they eventually settle arise out of a complex network of discovered information. As our learners collaborate with each other and technical experts to produce this idea, the complexity of the intertwining of ideas leads to a better result than any individual notion. This complex process leads to less of a surface-level learning approach, and, instead, increased academic performance is traced to higher retention of content and honing of essential skills.

> **Stage Three: Context and Perspective**
>
> How do we know if our learners have considered end-user needs and technical expert feedback?

The context of the challenge presents our learners with a fundamentally complex situation. A solution that may work in one condition won't work in another. That same resolution that is appropriate for one end-user audience won't satisfy another. Moreover, the time in which our learners craft the solution impacts its development. If an established solution only works for the foreseeable future, our learners have ignored a major complex element. Therefore, our learners must peel back the layers of the challenge to meet the needs of the presented context.

From here, our learners improve and fine-tune their ideas as they receive feedback from experts, peers, and us. This feedback, in turn, initiates further inquiry, as the complexity of this process often necessitates a return to Stage Two. Furthermore, each perspective enhances their concept, as they contemplate the benefits from each viewpoint. As our learners consider a variety of perspectives, they make improvements to their final ideas that ultimately result in a complex solution.

> **Stage Four: Actions and Consequences**
>
> How do we know if our learners have considered the potential positive and negative impacts of their proposed solution?

While it is relatively easy to suggest a solution without considering any potential effects, it is a complex process to view a proposed solution from the possible positive and negative outcomes that may result from its realization. Each action that results from an implemented solution has a consequence linked to it. These consequences may occur immediately or in the future. A fully developed solution must take into account a five-year, ten-year, and, for middle school learners, even a twenty-year projection is possible, that may result from the given answer. Each projected consideration into the future adds a tier of complexity.

If we have several teams of learners working toward the same resolution, now is the opportunity to have the teams compare their models and determine which one may be the best outcome for the challenge. As our learners make these comparisons, additional layers of complexity emerge as sometimes portions of one solution are combined with parts of another. If this result occurs, it is time to revisit Stages Two and Three for additional inquiry and feedback. This situation resolves issues in a class that intends to present to a panel of technical experts who may not have the time to listen to multiple offerings.

> **Stage Five: Options and Opportunities**
>
> How do we know if our learners have developed an actionable solution for their end-users?

When our learners develop a solution to present solely to their teacher and peers, we fundamentally strip complexity out of the experience. In that instance, there is no consideration for the end-user. However, once our learners express the pros and cons of each option they contemplated, they exhibit higher-level thinking at analysis and evaluation. Each option may be viable, however, whether or not each option is appropriate for the intended user is questionable. From here, our learners must justify to their authentic audience why they settled on the proposed solution, and why that audience should accept it as a feasible answer to the presented problem.

While our learners must come to a resolution for the challenge, as we have time constraints in the classroom, a genuinely complex challenge leaves the door open to future opportunities for refinement, remediation, and enhancements to the solution, which is similar to the process that smartphone developers go through as they improve their designs from year to year. Moreover, the challenge may present additional avenues for a new class to explore next year. These avenues allow you to recycle challenges without them losing their impact. A group of learners, the following year, may take the previous year's ideas and build upon them in some way. Additionally, some of our best challenges prompt our learners to continue the challenge past the given timeframe of the class investigation. Don't be surprised if you have a few or more enterprising young minds that continue to work on the challenge long after the grading concludes.

The multi-dimensional complexity that an authentic project experience has to offer our learners provides the prospect to potentially effect change in their world. Whether this change may or may not occur is less of a concern than the full process they engage in that leads to their empowerment as learners. Complexity promotes ownership in one's learning, as our adolescents and young teens envision the value they can contribute to their communities and beyond. This value imparts on them the importance of lifelong learning, and it solidifies their ability to offer solutions to complex challenges they will surely face in their adult lives.

Time to Reflect
1. What are the ways in which complexity can emerge in the challenge you have been developing?
2. What is an example of a complicated project you have implemented in the past, and how could you turn it into a complex learning experience?
3. How does the integration of your content standards and skills standards such as the ISTE ones described in Chapter 3 promote complexity in an authentic project?
Record Any Questions You Have Here

7

Essential Skills for Tomorrow

> How do we facilitate our learners' development of the essential skills needed to best prepare them for the world beyond school?

If you haven't already noticed, the preceding chapters of this book incorporated ideas and strategies on how to scaffold and facilitate communication, collaboration, critical thinking, and creativity. Twenty-first-century skills or soft skills are the commonly referenced terminology in education. I will argue, however, that communication, collaboration, critical thinking, and creativity are skills that have been important long before the 21st century. Moreover, these skills, while considered soft, are really **essential**, as those learners that do not strengthen them, will find themselves limited in many of their future endeavors. These labels, therefore, are outdated. While I will refer to these skills as essential throughout this chapter, their naming conventions, nevertheless, is a debate to which I'll leave you to ponder the merits. Instead, let's focus our efforts on how to move past this debate on to actionable changes for our classrooms. How do we facilitate our learners' development of the essential skills needed to best prepare them for the world beyond school?

If you have followed any of the work by the World Economic Forum, you know their Founder and Executive Chairman, Klaus Schwab, has intimated that we have already entered into what he calls the Fourth Industrial Revolution. This revolution is an era defined by technological advancements such as self-driving cars, quantum computing, and artificial intelligence, and these advancements continue to come to fruition at an exponential speed to "fuse the physical, digital, and biological worlds" (Schwab, 2016). Now, more than ever, to meet the economic, governmental, and environmental changes that accompany this revolution, it is imperative that we prepare our learners to live, work, and innovate in our globally connected world. Yet, in a survey jointly conducted by Deloitte and Global Business Coalition for Education (2018), over 50 percent of the students surveyed had never heard of the Fourth Industrial Revolution. Through authentic challenges, we have the opportunity to change this narrative.

Let's take a look at an example of the connection between the Fourth Industrial Revolution and the preparation of our learners for tomorrow. You probably can't remember very clearly a world in which recycling was not the norm. While some areas of the U.S. started recycling programs as early as the late 1960s, comprehensive plans for curbside pickup became available by the 1990s. Every week, millions of Americans put out their recycling bins after separating their acceptable plastics, papers, glass, and cans from the tons of garbage that ends up in our landfills and incinerators. (Already we have a challenge: How can we reduce the amount of waste in our landfills?) Most of the plastics we recycle have traditionally ended up on a ship bound for China. In fact, China's first female billionaire made her fortune in recycling America's discarded plastics. However, in early 2018, the Chinese government decided the value add of importing the world's unwanted (and almost impossible to recycle) contaminated plastic is no longer in their best interest as the profit margin has decreased while the negative environmental impact has increased. Thus, the more complex challenge for our learners is to figure out "How can we make recycling more profitable?"

From this example, we have an authentic challenge that is not only written in language that anyone can understand, but also is also one that requires our learners to use their skills for tomorrow to solve the challenge. We use this example throughout this chapter, in Tables 7.2 through 7.5, to illustrate how this challenge aligns to the Five Project Stages and our essential skills. (Please note that these tables have been modified and adapted to some degree from Laur & Ackers, 2017.)

The Fourth Industrial Revolution

In *Preparing Tomorrow's Workforce for the Fourth Industrial Revolution* (2018), the authors identified several categories of skills with examples of what is necessary to develop agile and adaptive learners who are ready for a future world of work that is ever changing. These skills include the most basic workforce readiness skills and level up to more nuanced essential or soft skills, technical skills, and entrepreneurship (Armstrong et al., 2018). Table 7.1 provides a more detailed list of what these noted skills include.

This entire book is about relevant, real-world challenges that require our learners to employ the skills necessary to become agile and adaptive learners. However, for our purposes in this chapter, let's align our challenges to the essential skills of collaboration, communication, critical thinking, and creativity to solve the authentic challenge. I think you will agree that the other skills listed in Figure 7.1 are embedded within and link to these skills. For example, grant writing requires well-developed communication skills, as well as presentation skills and cultural awareness. Furthermore, innovation and design thinking need critical thinking as a base skill set to propel our learners to a solutions-oriented approach to learning.

Ill-defined challenges provide our learners with the opportunity to personally define the problem and engage our learners in the chance to hone their critical thinking, collaboration, communication, and creativity prowess. Here, we must resist the desire to push our learners down a predetermined path toward our own formulated solution. Instead, as we ask our learners to define possible pathways to problems and find their answers, we immediately invite them to think critically rather than passively accept a solution devised by another. To do so, we must support our learners as they identify connections between the challenge and the relevance to their lives. This connection is imperative at this point as it activates a learner's prior knowledge and how it links to their understanding of newly introduced information. Here, the ways our learners take apart, reorganize, and rearrange the information related to the challenge requires the usage of all of the essential skills (Laur & Ackers, 2017).

Thus, we must deliberately include all of the essential skills into our planning. We cannot have one essential skill without the others, and it is necessary to assess each of them in all of the project stages. Through each stage, these required essential skills come through at a variety of levels of complexity. Additionally, the more frequently these essential skills are exercised, through engagement with a project-based learning experience, the deeper the firm foundation of practice becomes and translates into richer solutions to any challenge.

Table 7.1 Skills Necessary for the Fourth Industrial Revolution

	Identification	Need For	Examples
Workforce Readiness	Skills that are needed by our learners to help them successfully enter the job market once they leave K-12 education, if not before, go beyond textbook learning	The changing landscape of the job market over the next several decades requires a *work to learn* model rather than *learn to work* model of school.	♦ Presentation Skills ♦ Project Management ♦ Digital Literacy ♦ Work Ethic ♦ Numeracy
Essential/Soft Skills	Skills that require the ability to thrive in a social setting (face-to-face and digitally) with interpersonal relationships that are needed in the workplace	While digital connections will mainly continue to decrease the need for face-to-face and onsite interactions, virtual meetings and online communications are easier to misinterpret.	♦ Collaboration ♦ Communication ♦ Critical Thinking ♦ Cultural Awareness ♦ Adaptability
Technical Skills	Jobs of today and those jobs that have yet to be created require specialized skills that may be obtained outside of a traditional four-year college degree	As more instances of AI take over those tasks that are mundane in everyday job requirements, workers must become more specialized in their professions.	♦ Simplified Coding ♦ Design Thinking ♦ Financial Management ♦ Computational Literacy ♦ Job-Specific Understandings
Entrepreneurship	The ability to produce new information in a novel way that is desirable by others	The workforce of tomorrow requires a think outside of the box approach to be competitive on a global scale.	♦ Innovation ♦ Initiative ♦ Grant Writing ♦ Creative Thinking ♦ Curiosity

Since our primary goal is to design, or co-design with our learners and technical experts, an authentic project-based learning experience at the creation level of Bloom's, we automatically call for the highest level of critical thinking. Additionally, while most traditional unit projects never go beyond Bloom's application level, a genuinely open-ended authentic challenge propels our learners to the level of creation from the outset. It is then that our scaffolded lessons and connections with resources and experts support our learners' critical thinking and creativity at each stage. We must not forget, however, that these supports are not intended to design the solutions for our learners, nor should we have a preplanned solution that we either overtly or inadvertently present to our learners. It is the job of our learners to think critically to create a solution, and if we have done our job, our learners will do so because they found the challenge to be personally relevant to the degree that they were empowered to effect change through their proposed solution. Furthermore, our learners' collaboration and communication with one another, and with any technical experts, now becomes a more complex thinking process, as they refine their ideas, solutions, and prototypes through critical feedback.

Before we dive into each of our essential skills, let's take a moment to consider how many skills we may want to assess throughout the challenge. While some PBL experts call for teaching and assessing one skill per project, no matter what the grade level, I respectfully disagree. It is crucial to teach and assess all essential skills in the context of every project and to do so at every stage of project assessment. The continued assessment paints a vivid picture of our learners' growth over time, and we can compare this growth from project to project. Moreover, our learners also have the ability to recognize which skills they need to work on and which skills they have moved beyond proficiency. Collectively, this picture of growth presents us with the data necessary to modify and differentiate our lessons, activities, and personalized support for each and every learner in our classroom.

Critical Thinking

One of the biggest mistakes I made when I first began a project-based learning approach in my classroom was to limit the critical thinking that was required. On reflection, I just had my learners complete unit projects that were research papers in disguise. The targeted level of Bloom's was in most cases, at best, application. Once in a while, I probably hit analysis. However, the more I came to understand that my learners were simply completing these projects for a grade (and most were completing them at the last minute), the more I realized the level of critical thinking was too low.

In Stage One of our Project Assessment, our learners must understand the project, its purpose, and the relevant connections they have to the challenge. Without these three ingredients, we gamble a risky bet that our learners will chart a pathway of confusion that leads to frustration. In a worst-case scenario, our learners won't invest in the project and shut down from the start. This scenario exhibits the point at which they ask, "Why do I need to know/do this?" As a result, many teachers and learners, alike, shy away from PBL.

To prevent this debacle, in the first stage, as we introduce the challenge, we want our learners to make links to any previous experiences they have had that connect to the challenge. This link guides the development of inquiry questions about the challenge. From these questions, our learners decide what information they will need to investigate, research they will need to conduct, and data they will need to collect to interact with the challenge. Our learners must also determine what new practices they might need to explore, and even how to envision the challenge, if it isn't a new idea, in a novel way. For example, a challenge on how to redevelop an abandoned property into a park might not be an entirely new concept for many. Our upper elementary learners have indeed spent time on the playground and may have delved into civics concepts of community. Our middle school adolescents receive persuasive writing instruction that helps with a project such as this. However, it is likely that our learners, no matter what grade level, have not had any exposure to abandoned properties and the economic and social impacts they have on a community. Thus, we want them to take their broader understanding and envision the challenge in ways they previously would not have.

This start of the inquiry process is a crucial part of critical thinking. In fact, as the project challenge requires our learners to create new content, they are practicing critical thinking. The creation of new content does not mean that your learners make up random solutions; rather, they use their research skills to analyze and evaluate existing information to justify any new applications of that information in the creation of an entirely new solution. If your challenge does not require the production of new content, you had better go back to the drawing board, as the level of critical thinking is far too low to qualify for an open-ended challenge.

While a low-level Bloom's problem might introduce entirely new information, an open-ended challenge requires our learners to move up each level of Bloom's as they engage in higher levels of critical thinking until they are ready to identify new pathways to explore. Then, the connections between their own experiences, the understandings of their peers, and those of any technical experts with whom they partner lead to even deeper and more meaningful solutions as our learners engage in each stage of the project. The inquiry process that starts in Stage One directs our learners to consider what data and information they will need to gather in Stage Two as they begin to ideate a tangible solution to the challenge. Here, our learners sharpen their critical thinking skills as they begin to formulate creative solutions and think about ways to communicate them.

This connection to personal and relevant experiences starts with the first project stage and progresses through each remaining stage of the project, no matter how many times they cycle through each stage. We help our learners make these connections through the challenge launch to spark their inquiry and get them to ask questions about the challenge from the very beginning. We then facilitate the process for them to uncover the connections they may have through a variety of teacher tools that may include reflection prompts and collaborative discussion protocols such as Agreement Circles or Café Conversations. The regular incorporation of these types of tools and activities (see Appendix 1 for additional ideas) into our daily lessons allow for multiple pathways for our learners to demonstrate their critical thinking skills.

In Stage Two, as our learners make sense of the information, research, and data they have gathered, they are required to think critically about that evidence and how it might provide a justification for their proposed solution ideas at this juncture. Here, our learners are rooted in the process of inquiry. During this stage, they ask new questions and identify both pertinent and non-germane information that provides structure as they consider possible ideas for development. Our learners also interpret data points and begin to analyze their meaning. This research and data are then categorized into patterns as our learners start to ideate their first possible solutions or products. As our learners continue to engage in inquiry, their research and collected data leads to additional questions, enabling them to further refine and develop their ideas through determined and necessary adjustments and modifications. This revision process also hones their critical thinking skills as they determine what is possible, what won't fit the bill, and what makes the most sense as a solution.

We know most of our preteens, and young teenagers need us to help increase the size of their world to one that is meaningful but still manageable. Thus, a collaborative learning environment is imperative. In Stage Three, critical thinking requires our learners to consider a variety of perspectives and calls for our learners to compare, contrast, make judgments, and complete evaluations (Laur & Ackers, 2017). By this stage, our learners should fully understand the context challenge and their end goal they aspire to achieve. To demonstrate mastery of the context of the problem, our learners develop a web of understanding from the research and data they gather from the questions they generate, and they begin to synthesize the compilation of their findings from their inquiries. They have to figure out why they concur with or deviate from individually presented perspectives from their peers and, more importantly, from the authentic feedback from technical experts. Based on this feedback and differing perspectives, they must choose a pathway of inquiry and ideas, as they move into Stage Four.

Generally, in a traditional classroom, preteens and young teenagers are inclined to hurriedly complete a task rather than examine the possible consequences of their actions. In this stage, the mere request that they stop, pause, and consider potential outcomes requires critical thinking. If they take action on a proposal, then this likely consequence is a genuine possibility. Therefore, it is necessary for our learners to weigh all of the possible positive and negative impacts of their proposed solution. Here, the use of a SCAMPER (substitute, combine, adapt, modify, put to another use, eliminate, reverse) model to refine their solution aids their ability to complete this stage. The SCAMPER model is the very definition of divergent thinking and requires critical thinking for its successful completion (Laur & Ackers, 2017).

Once our learners complete the SCAMPER model or any other applicable activity or protocol (see Appendix 1 for additional ideas), it is time to shift their critical thinking to the option that provides them with the most opportunity for the challenge. In Stage Five, evaluation, the second-highest level of Bloom's, is apparent. Once our learners figure out the consequences of their determined solution, they must consider whether or not that solution is an actionable one that has the potential to effect change on their audience, end-user, or client. Moreover, here, they must contemplate how the outcomes of their solution will impact the end-user. For example, when Apple develops a new iPhone, they must consider the positive and negative implications for making a phone larger. At what point does the consumer say that a phone is too large for a mobile device, and what are the tradeoffs they are willing to accept for the increase in size?

In Stage Five, we require an explanation of how and why our learners arrived at their conclusion from the variety of options they considered throughout the project process. They must ponder all options before they finalize their solution to the challenge. Ultimately, the solution itself has reached the creation level of Bloom's. If, for some reason, you notice the solution has not reached this level, chances are your challenge was not written at the creation level. An example of this might be a series of tri-fold posters that list low-level Bloom's information for your audience to peruse.

Throughout each stage, it is imperative that we support our learners as they make their thinking visible to the point at which it has the potential to become a reality. This visible thinking is the basis for our Five Stages of Project Assessment, as we have the ability at each stage to refine, tweak, or replace lessons, activities, and individualized support to ensure each and every one of our learners can be successful as they engage in the challenge. Thus, we must ensure we embed many of the formative assessment strategies discussed in Chapter 5 and the additional options reviewed in Appendix 1. Visible thinking also encourages our learners to become aware of and reflect on their thinking as it evolves and matures. This refined and developed ability to think critically is the first intersection of a successful approach to an authentic project-based learning experience that prepares our learners for the world outside of the classroom (Laur & Ackers, 2017).

Table 7.2 Critical Thinking

Stages	Critical Thinking Link	Critical Thinking Example
Challenge and Purpose	♦ Relate the project challenge to personal experiences ♦ Connect the information they already know to the research they need to uncover	Learners connect the information they already know to the information they need to discover and ask inquiry questions related to the challenge: (i.e.) *How much does recycling cost?* *What can and can't we recycle?* *How do you make money off of recycling programs?*
Inquiry and Ideas	♦ Identify patterns in the information learned ♦ Troubleshoot ideas to figure out what is working and what is not	Learners investigate multiple databases, collect their own data, and research a variety of primary and secondary sources related to recycling.
Context and Perspective	♦ Weigh the value of the challenge in relation to the bigger picture of the overall topic ♦ Evaluate and then explain why they agree with a certain perspective and disagree with other perspectives	Learners identify patterns in their collected data as they align with any research from additional sources and identify why any outliers exist in the data.
Actions and Consequences	♦ Determine "if … then …" statements ♦ Weigh the positives and negatives of potential consequences related to each action	Learners complete a pro/con chart of what they predict will happen in the present through three decades out if their recycling plan were implemented.
Options and Opportunities	♦ Evaluate the opportunity costs of their intended solution compared to the options they considered ♦ Envision the opportunities the solution will provide in the future	Learners must justify how they arrived at their solution and can answer on the spot questions from the panel of waste management experts.

Collaboration

Take a moment to reflect on your day. How many instances require you to collaborate in some form or another? Whether that partnership comes in the form of team teaching in your classroom or directly working with your teaching peers in your grade level team regularly, you understand what it means to be a good colleague. The experience of being a good colleague doesn't mean you haven't also had your share of trials as you work together. In fact, any struggles you may have faced can help you to shape the collaborative work required in an authentic learning experience. Hopefully, you have also had the good fortune to exchange ideas with someone outside of your comfort zone. Perhaps you have connected with an educator from another district that you met in an online class or have forged a partnership with a technical expert who has strengthened your planning for a project. In any case, you already have many of the tools necessary to support collaboration building with your learners.

Collaboration is much more than merely putting learners into teams. In fact, many parents, teachers, and kids decry PBL due to misaligned ideas about what collaboration entails. So, let's set the record straight right now. Collaboration in a project does not mean you must put your learners in teams! Furthermore, I'm a firm believer that forcing learners into a team with predetermined roles complicates the collaborative process to a point at which it often fails. For example, assigning someone to be the researcher means that no one else in the group learns how to research, while another learner keeps their group members on task and has nothing to show in the way of content growth. Instead, if teams are a part of your planning process, let the roles emerge between your learners and ensure that all learners are responsible for participating in the portions of the project that require them to produce evidence of their learning.

There are plenty of instances in which you might want your learners to complete a project challenge as an individual. For example, as an art teacher, you probably wish to have everyone in your class paint, sculpt, or draw their own masterpiece. Similarly, as an ELA teacher, you might expect everyone to write his or her own short story. Of course, there are opportunities in both of these examples for our learners to collaboratively write or draw together; it just depends on the goals for the challenge. However, in each of these examples, your learners should have the opportunity to collaborate even if they are expected to produce an individual submission.

It is imperative to embed multiple occasions for our learners to collaborate with one another and with technical experts throughout the project process. This collaboration with adults empowers our learners to become active members of their community who believe they can effect change. However, since we must foster collaboration skills, especially when social and emotional skills are still developing in upper elementary and middle school grades, we need to model collaborative skills for our learners. Many of the activities and protocols described in Appendix 1 explicitly model these collaborative skills, and I encourage you to embed them as frequently as possible throughout the project. You can use these as peer-to-peer collaboration, similar to the implementation of Café Conversations. Although, you have the opportunity to structure technical expert interactions through these protocols, as well. For a learner-to-adult interaction, the use of a Think It Through activity is an example of how our technical experts bring the authentic context to the content of the project.

In the first stage of our project, it is essential that our learners immediately connect to the challenge. Often, our learners do this as they make links between previous personal experiences or prior knowledge. However, not every learner enters into the challenge with the same level of experience. Therefore, we must create a classroom environment that encourages the collaborative sharing of experiences so that our learners first begin to individually articulate and then, ultimately, co-create a series of inquiry questions they need to explore to tackle the challenge strategically. Once we set that foundation, the collaborative exploration of project materials develops a shared experience that propels the project forward (Laur & Ackers, 2017).

No matter what grade level we teach, we should not assume our learners know how to collaborate effectively. Therefore, we must provide guidance and tools to help them achieve their collaboration goal: complete a task, design an idea, or present a solution. The tools that support collaboration are necessary as even we, as adults, sometimes also struggle to collaborate without effective processes in place. You probably already know how the following scenario plays out. You and your grade level team are provided an afternoon of professional development time to work in small groups to work on a portion of your curriculum that is due for revision. Inevitably, someone takes the lead and starts assigning tasks to the remaining members of the team. One person is desperately trying to finish grades for progress reports that are due at the end of the day. Another person excuses himself or herself to attend an IEP meeting. And, a third person hops up after a half hour to attend a previously scheduled doctor's appointment, as they would rather miss PD time than class time. That leaves two of you to try and complete the work that was left behind by those that needed to attend to other issues. While no real fault lies with these teachers based on the limited time scheduled to complete the task, this scenario illustrates a very common problem with our own learners.

What if we instead provided a structure to the collaborative process to help improve our learners' skills? We might use the breakdown protocol in Stage One to have our learners initiate questions that they have about the challenge. Here, it is important to note that our learners do this process on an individual basis first. In the initial half of the process, learners list the steps they think are necessary to complete the challenge. From here, learners join their teams to share out the steps they imagine. Once an agreed-upon list exists, they then move back into an individual phase. The second half of the process has learners turn each step into a list of questions they believe must be answered. Once our learners finish this portion of the activity, again, they team up to compare their lists to generate a master list of inquiry questions. This individual list ensures everyone hears all ideas. Through this protocol, we have also completed a pre-assessment of our learners' understanding of the problem. Based on the steps they created and the questions they posed, as individuals, we have a window into their understanding of the challenge and can correct any misconceptions from the start. Additionally, we have a firm understanding of how we may need to start to scaffold lessons for our learners throughout the project.

Once our learners make the shift into Stage Two, it is even more important to facilitate effective collaboration between them. Even if you have developed a project that requires an individually completed end product, collaboration will serve you well here. Stage Two could go on for copious amounts of time that we don't have in the given confines of our daily schedules. We typically have between 45 and 90 minutes of class time with our learners for any given subject. Of course, at the upper elementary grades, we tend to modify our schedules as needed with our colleagues. At the middle school level, I have also witnessed very successful teams who divide their time between classes based on the tasks for each class as they relate to the given project. Thus, delving into research as our learners collect data and new information could go on endlessly, but that's generally given time we don't have to spend. However, if our learners collaborate to share their newly gained knowledge, we significantly reduce the amount of time needed in the first part of this stage. Here, we may want to set up an online repository where they can share their findings with their group or, if you'd like, with the class. Google Classroom provides the perfect location for these resources. However, you can use any number of learning management systems or other free sites to collect, sort, and manage the shared research.

This joint research effort helps our learners to produce more fully developed preliminary ideas. If your learners are working in groups to produce an answer to the challenge, I would still suggest you have them individually create their initial ideas at this juncture. Again, this is the perfect opportunity for you to formatively assess their understanding and learning. Of course, the end goal of the team idea is a collective of several individual ideas. This collection of ideas is one of the benefits of collaboration, as the sum of the whole is better than the individual parts. From here, the groups have the opportunity to choose the best plan or prototype for moving forward into Stage Three. Although, please note, if you decide to go the individual route, such as in the art and ELA example I previously mentioned, you still have plenty of opportunity for collaboration in Stage Three.

Once our learners have a working idea, they shift into Stage Three. Here, it is time for them to receive feedback from you and their peers initially. You may want to introduce a protocol such as the Feedback Carousel, developed by the National School Reform Faculty and described in Appendix 1. This feedback is taken into consideration, and it is possible they may need to loop back to Stage Two to make adjustments to their ideas or prototypes.

From this working idea, teacher and peer feedback is only enough of a perspective to slightly shift our learners' ideas into a more feasible one. As your learners move deeper into Stage Three, technical experts will better understand the context of their proposed solution. During this round of feedback, these technical experts present an entirely new perspective for our learners to consider. Additionally, with a move into Stage Four, our technical experts provide valuable insight into the positive or negative implications of a possible solution from the perspective of someone in the field. This insight is, of course, more valuable in the eyes of our learners, and rightfully so. While we can provide educational perceptions, unless we have worked in the field our learners are exploring in the context of the challenge, we don't have the level of knowledge and proficiency that matches that of a technical expert.

When teamed, our learners enter into the final stage during which they apply any finishing touches in preparation for the moment they share their challenge solutions with their authentic audience. Here, collaboratively contributed ideas and feedback enhance the solution. However, if an individual focus is a required approach to your project, you can still incorporate a collaborative aspect to Stage Five. If the final product/solution is presented to an audience, there should be an element of collaborative conversation between your learners and the end-users. If you have no formal presentation planned, collaboration can still happen if they request a final feedback response. This information can possibly then be used for future classes of learners who may work on the same or a similar project. In some cases, learners may continue to pursue the challenge beyond the confines of the classroom timetable.

Before we move on, I would be remiss if I didn't note that not every authentic project experience has to be a team effort. There are plenty of opportunities to incorporate collaborative occasions into the challenge without a team approach to the end product. As mentioned earlier in this section, collaboration with technical experts or peer review opportunities enhance our learners' abilities to work with others.

Communication

An environment of open dialog in a classroom is typically limited to the occasional debate or Socratic Seminar in which learners are encouraged to

Table 7.3 Collaboration

Stages	Collaboration Link	Collaboration Example
Challenge and Purpose	♦ Share personal experiences related to the challenge ♦ Partner with technical experts for a first exploration of the challenge	Class partners with a local recycling center to launch the project either with an onsite visit to the center or a classroom visit.
Inquiry and Ideas	♦ Combine research and data gathered ♦ Merge varying individual ideas to produce a workable team idea	Work with a recycling or conservation specialist to collect data on recycling.
Context and Perspective	♦ Conduct a discussion activity to share and compare ♦ Receive feedback from technical experts	Collaborate with peer groups from different parts of the country (or world) that experience a variety of recycling-related issues in order to cull the best points of view in the development of a collaborative solution that is viable for local, as well as global communities.
Actions and Consequences	♦ Role-play actions and the potential consequences that may result ♦ Provide an action and have a partner write a possible consequence for that action	A series of feedback sessions between learners and recycling experts lead to refined prototypes.
Options and Opportunities	♦ Evaluate all the possible solutions that each team member has proposed before finalizing a solution ♦ Collaborative presentation to share with the authentic audience	Learners immediately respond to the summative feedback provided by the panel of recycling experts and make a plan to incorporate that feedback into their proposal in preparation for implementation.

converse for a limited amount of time on a narrow topic. Written communication is generally completed as a graded experience in the form of an essay or the occasional short story. Conversely, authentic challenges provide a learning ecosystem that allows us to foster and model open avenues of communication. When we allow for these interactions in our classrooms, we bring our learners together through discussion to inextricably link collaboration with communication in Stage One. The task, grade level of our learner, or the purpose of the project ultimately affects the result of how our learners articulate their learning.

Without a focus on communication, we limit the skills of critical thinking and collaboration, in their isolation, as stand-alone. From the start, our learners must communicate their interpretation of the challenge. This interpretation takes place in both oral and written form. Here, I encourage you to implement the ideas discussed in Chapter 4 for initiating the inquiry process. As our learners develop their initial inquiry questions, it is a pre-assessment of their understanding of the challenge. In essence, this is how our learners inform us about the supports they may need us to provide through scaffolded lessons. This is a much different experience than taking a pre-assessment in the form of a quiz. Instead, we covertly uncover the needs of our learners, and how we will support them now becomes a joint endeavor instead of a one-sided decision (Laur & Ackers, 2017).

As our learners move deeper into Stage One, they articulate a project plan. Here, we have several options for how we might ask them to communicate this plan. One of my favorites is the use of Scrumy (scrumy.com). The use of Scrumy breaks down the challenge into what learners need to accomplish throughout the project in a series of "stories." If you team your learners for the project, Scrumy provides the format to assign team members tasks or stories to complete. Within Scrumy, our learners now communicate with one another how they are accomplishing their project plans. A quick look at their Scrumy table also communicates with us what they have accomplished, what they need, and where they are going next. Please note that you can also have your learners complete this in an analog format. If you do not have access to digital devices on a regular basis, a chart paper/post-it note version of Scrumy is just as effective.

The inquiry questions our learners initiate in Stage One lead to the Stage Two articulation of answers through research and data gathering. These answers provide them with the initial context from which they start building their ideas of potential solutions. As our learners articulate these ideas with their peers, us, and, eventually technical experts, they reveal their thought processes. Here, it is an excellent idea to formatively assess their understanding of the challenge and any misconceptions that may have sprouted during their research. We want to ensure we head off these misconceptions before our learners get too deep into this stage. Of course, trial and error is the hallmark of Stage Two as revisions emerge through new thinking related to the inquiry process.

In Stage Three, it is time for our learners to articulate their ideas and opinions related to the challenge. They must also practice their communication skills with technical experts who may present a very different perspective on the challenge. This skillset also requires our learners to critically think about how the perspectives overlap with their personal thinking, while pushing them to consider the context in which the solution is meant for application. Depending on the responses from the technical experts, our learners may have to loop back to Stage Two. Within Stage Three, for our later elementary learners, this is an opportunity for them to articulate the comparisons of different perspectives on the challenge and possible solutions in the form of a fictional story. This twist on communication intertwines multiple essential skills and provides us with an additional formative check for understanding before our learners move on to Stage Four (Laur & Ackers, 2017).

We must also remember, it can be a scary thing for a young child to talk to another person. The same is true for some of our quieter middle school teens. Practice presentations and the inclusion of experts in the middle of the project afford them the time to enhance their communication skills. This feedback from Stage Three is intended to cause our learners to pause and consider the potential effects of their actions. While this can be a reflective activity through journaling or a more open communication through a fishbowl activity, this is the point at which our learners are expected to be able to communicate the consequences of their solutions. They must be

Table 7.4 Communication

Stages	Communication Link	Communication Example
Challenge and Purpose	♦ Ask initial inquiry questions about the challenge ♦ Articulate a plan of what must be accomplished in the challenge	Learners describe how the recycling challenge affects their community and how it impacts them as consumers of plastic products.
Inquiry and Ideas	♦ Devise interview or survey questions ♦ Explain the evolution of the ideation process	Learners conduct a survey of local citizens through carefully worded questions intended to elicit important information. Similarly, interviews can take the place of surveys.
Context and Perspective	♦ Explain the way in which the challenge affects the local community in comparison to a more national or global approach ♦ Explain the overlap and differences discovered between offered perspectives	Learners articulate a devised plan of action for how to tackle the challenge over the course of the project and receive feedback from a recycling technical expert.
Actions and Consequences	♦ Ask others what they think might be the results of the implemented solution ♦ Discuss the design changes throughout the project and why they were made	Learners relay to recycling experts their justification for their chosen course of action and discuss with these experts their offered feedback to make improvements to their solution.
Options and Opportunities	♦ Use charts, graphs, or diagrams to support their solution ♦ Justify their end solution to their authentic audience	Learners clearly present their final idea to a panel of experts such as waste management experts, state department of environmental protection members, or local university economics professors.

convincing by this stage, as our learners need to communicate the changes they made to their designs throughout the project and explain why they implemented those changes and the potential positive and negative outcomes of those changes.

Our final stage requires our learners to justify their solutions to their authentic audience as they reveal the options they considered and the opportunities presented by the proposed solution. Whether as an oral presentation or through written communication, here, the use of charts, graphs, or diagrams visually communicates the data used to support their determined outcomes for the opportunities they present if and when enacted. Here our learners express their understanding of the content and mastery of the standards. As a conclusion to the project experience, a shared story about learning emerges. This story is one that is more meaningful than any flawlessly scored test our learners could ever have completed.

Creativity

Creativity is the highest level of the revised Bloom's Taxonomy. We engage in this level, as we create an authentic project-based learning experience for our learners (Laur & Ackers, 2017). The challenge itself is written at the level of creativity, and, thus, requires our learners to also engage in creativity. In Stage One, our learners begin to identify the unique attributes of the challenge as they define their purpose for solving the problem. However, creativity is often mistaken for a visually appealing product. This mistake aligns with the traditional projects we discussed in Chapter 1. The "creation" of that book trailer video describing why someone should read the book, is actually a research paper in disguise that is lower-level Bloom's work. Conversely, the definition of creativity as it relates to our authentic project challenges is the development of something original. But, wait, Dayna! Can't a video on a book summary be creative with background music and graphics?

A quick way to check for the desired high-level Bloom's creativity is to see if the idea passes the NUF test, which is a simple test used in the world of patenting. To apply the NUF test, you simply rank how new, useful, and feasible the idea is in relation to the challenge. With the application of this test, it is easy to see that the video example does not receive high scores on the NUF test. However, the recycling challenge woven throughout this chapter passes the NUF test at a much higher threshold. While the NUF test works for us as we design challenges, the NUF test can also be applied to our learners' ideas as they begin Stage Two when they start to formulate initial ideas born out of their inquiry, research, and data collection. Here, agile learners have the premier opportunity to engage in the creative process.

An example of creativity, shared in Laur and Ackers (2017), that propels our users beyond the first and second stage and into further development of their initial ideas is through the use of the Reversal Technique. This technique is a creative process that challenges our learners to improve their solutions. In Stages Three and Four, to empower our learners to refine their ideas, we ask them how they could cause the problem. From here, we have them brainstorm ideas on how to change behaviors that cause the problem in the first place. This sparks ideas on how to solve the actual challenge and gives us an opportunity to have our learners think outside of the box and employ an empathetic approach to the challenge. A slightly different approach to the Reversal Technique is to have our learners explain the reverse of their product design. The reversal means they start from the end product and trace the steps back to the problem. This creative twist helps to bring to light any gaps in their design process.

Creativity, at its core, is the ability to take a fresh look at a problem, product, or challenge. Our learners must be ready to assimilate unique ideas and apply them to their solution for the challenge, as they take two or more previously unconnected problem elements and combine them to make something that works (Laur & Ackers, 2017). This combination is where context comes into play for Stage Three. Depending on the context in which the solution is to be applied, it may or may not work. Moreover, what might work in one setting for a given user may not work for another. Thus, we must challenge our learners to picture the problem from multiple perspectives. A role-play activity is appropriate here before consulting with technical experts.

As our learners realize the context of the challenge, they also come to realize that an open-ended problem allows for any number of actionable solutions. Thus, in Stage Four, as our learners consider the potential consequences of their actions, they convert possible negative effects into positive ones. Similarly, you can have your learners do the reverse, in which positive consequences are turned into negative ones to deepen the critical thinking and creativity of the solution, all the while considering possible consequences from their actions.

While a creatively designed presentation might catch the attention of the audience, it is not enough to convince them that the solution presented should be an accepted one. Rather, the truly creative aspect is exhibited through a combination of seemingly separate ideas into an innovative single solution. A presentation, however, can take many forms and isn't necessarily the stand and deliver model. In fact, you already know I am not a fan of the typical presentations of learning (POLs). These exhibition nights are more often showcases of low-level Bloom's work that do little to consider the actionable impacts of the solution for the end-user. Thus, we regard even a letter to the editor as an authentic presentation. If, however, you and your learners decide a formal panel presentation is appropriate, having an authentic audience in the presence of your learners levels up the experience for them. Here, our learners creatively communicate their ideas as they convince their audience of the plausibility of their conclusions (Laur & Ackers, 2017).

As our learners develop, assess, refine, and master their essential skills, we must also build an agile and adaptive ecosystem that prepares our

Table 7.5 Creativity

Stages	Creativity Link	Creativity Example
Challenge and Purpose	◆ Ask questions that exhibit out-of-the-box thinking ◆ Suggest an approach to the challenge that was not an original intent of the teacher's design	Learners might shift from an initially intended economic policy approach to an environmental viewpoint to solve the challenge.
Inquiry and Ideas	◆ Ask questions that refocus the challenge in a unique way ◆ Meld disparate ideas as a workable solution	Learners investigate and evaluate recycling efforts from a variety of regions in the U.S. and abroad.
Context and Perspective	◆ Apply a solution from a different context into the current context, using innovative tweaks ◆ Conduct interviews of technical experts in other fields that may not overtly relate to the topic but, upon further investigation, provide insight into the challenge	Learners select to interview an energy expert, industrial ecology expert, and solid waste expert in addition to the recycling experts already identified by the teacher.
Actions and Consequences	◆ Predict how the actions of today will impact the future ◆ Take the possible negative consequences and turn them into positive possibilities	Learners prepare a statement of how to deal with any negative effects of their proposed recycling plan.
Options and Opportunities	◆ Design an innovative solution to the challenge ◆ See the future extension of the challenge past the proposed solution	Learners design a follow-up study to the challenge for next year's class to tackle.

learners for the future world of work. To achieve this ecosystem, there are fundamental points we can't ignore.

1. Our learners bring diverse experiences to our classroom.
2. The intersection of required standards, essential skills, and, most importantly, authentic challenges develop a classroom experience that relates to our learners in a meaningful way.
3. Our adolescents learn differently, and we can't expect them to learn the way we, as teachers, prefer to learn and teach.
4. The adaptability and agility of our learners' minds is an asset in any classroom as they have the gift to think outside of the box in ways we may not even imagine.
5. All learners can develop their essential skills for growth in every challenge they tackle.

Writing this book, for me, was a journey that began years ago as a young learner who figured out the game of school. I didn't like to collaborate because I always ended up being in charge of the project. Communication was something that I likened to torture, as I hated getting up in front of the class. And, we might as well forget critical thinking and creativity since I simply memorized everything I needed to know for a test. That journey continued through my early years as an educator who desperately wanted to make my classroom a student-centric one that supported the building of all essential skills in my students. As I plodded through my first years of teaching, staying one step ahead of my learners, I began to dabble in PBL. My first attempts at projects are ones for which I would like to apologize. While they championed collaboration and communication, they severely lacked critical thinking and creativity, but I learned so much from each of them. As I moved into more of an authentic learning experience space, I found myself connecting with educators and technical experts from all over the world. It was on this part of the journey that I met Jill Ackers, and we took a few years, together, to develop the initial version of the Five Stages to Finding a Solution. During that time, we co-authored *Developing Natural Curiosity: 5 Strategies for the PreK-3 Classroom*. I couldn't have written that book without her, as her experience at the early elementary level was invaluable.

For this portion of my journey, this book was mostly a personal labor of love, as I struggled to also work on writing my dissertation while running Project ARC with Tim Kubik, my partner, not to mention being mom to Claire and Lydia, and a wife to Eric. Many of the ideas for this book were born out of the work that Jill and I did from 2014 to mid-2018. I borrowed chart structures, sentences, and an occasional paragraph or two from several of the chapters in our book, as I'm sure you noticed. The reflections at the end of each chapter that Jill believed were so important are somewhat of a departure from our original thinking, and instead have been refined into targeted questions related to each chapter. Additionally, some of the chapters in this book followed original formats from our book, while other chapters were almost a complete departure.

The Five Stages have been adapted and refined, as all good work continues to morph as we grow as individuals. Thanks, in part, to my collaboration with Tim Kubik, three of the five stages have been renamed. I also rewrote the questions related to each stage. And, the "ah-ha" moment that Tim discovered was a departure from approaching the stages through a design lens. Instead, we decided an assessment lens is more appropriate for understanding the implementation process of any authentic learning experience. This refinement and revision are part of the critical thinking and creative process. Based on this experience, I am confident my thoughts will continue to change in the coming years as I work more with technical experts from a variety of student-centric organizations. For all of this, I am thankful.

While there is one final chapter to this book that consists of a series of questions and answers, this chapter is, in effect, the end of this journey. However, I, too, know you are each on a personal journey of developing authentic challenges for your learners. For that, I wish you the best of luck as you seek to empower your learners and shift your classroom ecosystems from a passive *learn to work* model to a *work to learn* model of problem-solvers. Authentic project experiences create an intertwined network of community assets and draw on the experiences of technical experts to support our learners in ways that reinforce the essential skills every learner possesses and desperately wants to develop in a meaningful way.

As a collective group of readers of this book and dedicated educators, I know we all want every learner to successfully transition from our classrooms to the world outside of school with the ability to think critically, communicate, collaborate, and be creative at whatever they choose to do in life. As Jill and I noted in our first book, there is an art to this development of a young generation of problem-solvers. It is our responsibility to sustain their ability to ask "why" over and over again as they embark on their personal journeys and define their educational stories.

Time to Reflect

1. What is the learner impact of incorporating an authentic project-based learning experience that involves all aspects of an essential skillset necessary for the Fourth Industrial Revolution?

2. How do you intend to allow each of the essential skills to emerge in each stage of the authentic challenge you have been developing as you read this book?

3. How will you account for differentiation regarding each essential skill as needed for each of your learners?

Record Any Questions You Have Here

8

Commonly Asked Questions about PBL

If you are one of those readers who like to explore the end of the book before diving into the meat of the story, this chapter is for you. Perhaps, instead, you are a reader who takes copious notes, but you still have some lingering questions. If so, this chapter is also for you! In any case, over the last decade of partnering with districts to coach, guide, and facilitate PBL professional learning sessions, there are quite a few questions that I hear regularly. I've compiled those questions in this chapter for a quick reference guide.

I've assigned projects before, how is PBL different?

A basic project takes place at the end of a unit when all of the teaching has ended. Often a project is a summative assessment of the learning that took place throughout that unit. Sometimes, the project replaces a unit test. On occasion, a project is implemented before a holiday break or in the last week or two of school.

While I have at some points in this book mentioned projects as an all-encompassing reference to the authentic, relevant, and complex challenges I define as PBL, there is a distinct difference. Project-based learning, as I define it, is an inquiry-based approach to the discovery of new ideas that have the potential to effect change with a problem solution. Here, we begin with an open-ended challenge that has no one right answer before we start with the teaching. However, we must also launch the process of inquiry, as we launch the challenge.

This launch requires us to pique the interest of our learners, as they immediately see the relevance of the challenge and begin to ask questions. These questions serve as our pre-assessment of our learners' understanding of the problem. We know the purpose of the challenge is clear to our learners when they connect with the end-user for whom the solution will ultimately impact. Thus, the learning becomes a process with an end-goal focus that evolves into a story of learning, rather than a scripted activity that has a predetermined outcome.

I have seen some example PBL videos and read a few articles online about PBL examples, isn't this just a form of community service?

There are lots of examples on the Internet categorized as PBL. You have to be judicious in your evaluation of these examples, as many may purport to be PBL, when, in fact, they are research papers in disguise. These are end of the unit, essay test questions turned into a more extended version of a scripted activity. However, sometimes projects have little to no bearing on the content or standards in a course.

Frequently, a community service idea comes to fruition in a classroom with well-intentioned project ideas. However, community service is best left for an afterschool club to tackle. If you can't determine how to interweave your standards and content in the idea, chances are it is merely a feel-good project. The idea of picking up trash on the side of the road more than likely doesn't relate to your course. Similarly, raising money for cancer research doesn't elevate the complexity of the challenge. While your learners may not be trying to find a cure for cancer, the fact that we don't have a cure is the complex challenge, while raising money to support cancer research is a complicated endeavor.

I spent all of this time planning a challenge, can I use this project idea again?

Without a doubt, challenge ideas are recyclable (no pun intended). Each group of learners that walk through your doorway is different; therefore, they will bring different ideas and pathways for exploration to the challenge. You can run a project ten times over and have ten very different outcomes. Furthermore, depending on the result of the challenge, a new pathway may open up for a slightly different variation of the challenge. You may, however, find that you get bored with the same project idea and want to change it up.

Each new day brings a plethora of opportunities to develop a challenge. As I mentioned in Chapter 2, your learners may come to you with a challenge that was sparked by any number of interests they may reveal. Otherwise, a news article that you read might ignite an idea for a fresh learning experience. For some of you, you may opt to keep the same challenge multiple times with only a slight twist. Just know that there is no one right way to go about it and that is part of the authentic challenge we face as we shift our pedagogical approach in the classroom.

I can envision struggles when I implement PBL, what do I do if a project is a failure?

There are bound to be unexpected turns in your PBL journey, and each new project with every class has the potential to present you with any number of unexpected events. If you have the time and are motivated enough to try, you can always work through the challenge on your own to anticipate possible issues. However, more than likely, if you do attempt a dry run of sorts, you may unknowingly be inclined to push some of your ideas onto your learners. Of course, this is something that you want to avoid, so be acutely aware of this conceivable situation.

It is also critical to note that an open-ended challenge that allows for complex pathways of discovery can also lead to unanticipated outcomes. These unanticipated outcomes aren't necessarily a bad situation. PBL is messy on many fronts, and you need to be comfortable with that type of learning environment. It takes time to adjust, as both a teacher and a learner, so don't be unduly hard on yourself.

One of the best ways to ensure you head off any issues that may arise is to ensure you have included as many opportunities for formative assessments as possible throughout each stage of the project. In Stage One, it is imperative that you make sure your learners all understand the purpose of the challenge before moving forward. This assurance will likely head off any potential failure before your learners get too deeply ingrained with a misconception about the goals of the project.

If you do find yourself in a situation in which the PBL experience is causing quite a bit of angst for your learners, there is nothing wrong with stopping and regrouping. Here, you can try a Socratic Seminar with an affinity mapping session to cull out the issues at hand. However, there may be an occasion in which you need to cut your losses – it happens to the best of us. You should not, however, witness crying or angry learners. If you do, it is likely time to walk away from the project before the situation gets worse or your learners will shut down. If these types of exhibited emotions are the norm, it is unlikely that much learning is happening anyway. Instead, use it as a teachable moment and debrief the situation. Your learners will trust and thank you more in the end.

If I create an interdisciplinary project and ask other teachers to join, what kind of a project commitment should I expect from those teachers?

One of the biggest failures I had, as I shifted to a PBL pedagogical approach, was when I developed an interdisciplinary project on my own and then invited another teacher to implement it with me. On paper and in theory it sounds like a great idea. However, since I did not encourage the other teacher to co-design the challenge with me, he was not invested in the project. There was no ownership of the learning experience from his perspective, and on reflection, that project was doomed from the start.

Once you get an idea for an interdisciplinary challenge, talk it over with your colleagues. The more input you request, the more likely the other teacher or teachers will buy into what you are selling. Moreover, the idea for the challenge will have multiple perspectives and will enrich the challenge.

Of course, an interdisciplinary PBL experience can have varying levels of involvement from one or more teachers. The content area driving the project will frame the involvement. For example, your social studies class may need a significant statistical data analysis completed for the validation of the solution. More than likely, you won't have a class full of statisticians, and it isn't in your content standards to teach statistics. Here, you would want to bring in a stats class for that one portion of the project. While, in other cases, it could be a fully integrated approach in which all content areas share the responsibility equally.

If all of the teachers in my school adopt a PBL approach, won't my learners get overwhelmed with too many projects to complete?

A genuine PBL ecosystem should not require learners to complete their projects at home. In fact, you may consider eliminating all homework once you shift to a fully PBL systemic change. If anything, your learners might create their homework based on their excitement and desire to continue working on a project.

As you get started on your PBL journey, you may want to connect with your teaching partners to discuss upcoming projects to ensure you don't have due dates that collide for presentations or scheduled field work. In fact, in some instances, you might find that there are overlaps with your projects that could extend into other classrooms for additional support. There is no requirement for this, however.

I have even scheduled two simultaneous projects within my classroom. I developed one project with a cadre of other teachers from around the country. We had a full twelve weeks to complete the project but did not need all of that allotted time. The timetable was designed to meet the needs of all classes with scheduled breaks and state testing dates that we had to take into consideration. Therefore, I ran that project every Monday for twelve weeks, and on the other four days of the week my learners focused on a different project from a separate unit. At first, I was tentative on how it would logistically pan out and was worried about possible confusion with due dates between the two schedules. My worry was unfounded, however, as my learners seamlessly transitioned between the two projects.

I want to make authentic, relevant, and complex learning catch on in my school, how do I do this?

All it takes is one successful authentic challenge for your learners to spread the word. Even the most resistant teachers begin to take notice when they hear the whisperings of what Mr./Mrs. So and So has going on in their classroom. Additionally, an opportunity to contact your district's PR department to connect you with the news media or to showcase an article on the school website builds momentum.

In this case, an authentic approach to learning becomes homegrown. Now there is no need to try to visit a showcased site halfway across the country or by watching videos on various educational sites. Consequently, your colleagues can't claim that it won't work in your building!

I co-teach my class with a special education teacher, how will we differentiate a challenge to ensure all of our learners complete the challenge successfully?

All great open-ended challenges naturally lead to differentiation. This inherent differentiation is a prime opportunity for you to include all of your IEP learners, no matter what their reading level or what extra support they need. More than likely, you may also have unidentified learners in your classroom that would benefit from additional modifications.

The trick is to ensure that you use your co-teacher as a true co-teacher. Please don't relegate your co-teacher to only assisting their IEP learners. Similarly, don't call out your IEP learners to be in a group together for the project or for small group activities. Instead, the best co-teachers play off of one another during class as they run mini-lessons, small group sessions, or coach learners individually. The seamless transition between the two of you gives you both equal weight in the classroom.

My school has a high population of English Language Learners, will I still be able to use PBL in my classroom?

As noted in the answer to the question above, an open-ended challenge allows for differentiation for all learners. As our ELLs may have varying degrees of language acquisition needs, you can decide what modifications to the challenge may be necessary for them. (This advice is also suitable for any of your IEP learners when needed.) Work with your ELL teacher for assistance when necessary.

For your more proficient ELLs, you may only need to make minor modifications with reading options. On the other hand, you may also have a learner that is communicating with pictures only. When needed, you may have to adjust any requirements that you have for the project. Short written conditions are frequently acceptable here.

Several of the strategies listed in Chapter 5 as formative assessment options are from GLAD (Guided Language Acquisition Design). I call your attention to them here, as they support not only your ELLs but all learners. A co-op strip paragraph works well here. Thus, you can implement a GLAD strategy with a full class without calling attention to your ELLs.

I have heard that PBL is only appropriate for honors or gifted learners, what if I don't teach higher-level groups of learners?

From the above questions, you should have already gleaned that PBL is not just for our higher-level learners. Of course, if you only teach gifted learners or honors classes, PBL is an effective means to push them out of their comfort zone of often just wanting to know the right answer. This push out of a comfort zone can be a difficult proposition for your older learners that have figured out how to play the game of school effectively. In fact, our higher-scoring learners are frequently the ones who resist PBL the most adamantly, as they truly experience challenges in education for the first time.

The repeated theme in this book has explored how to write a launch question at the creation level of Bloom's. As the highest level of critical thinking, this automatically requires our learners to challenge themselves to innovate. In turn, this sentiment might seem like PBL is only appropriate for our higher-level learners. However, this is far from the case. Frequently, it is our lower-performing learners who outwardly realize the most benefit from a pedagogical shift in our classrooms.

Typically, lower-scoring learners don't do well on tests because they aren't good test takers. Memorization of information can be a difficult thing, but the inability to memorize facts and figures does not equate to intelligence level.

Thus, creating a classroom ecosystem in which all learners are challenged to create, rather than remember, information that one can quickly look up on their smartphone, develops learners who are far better prepared to participate in the world outside of school. No matter what the data reveals about each of our learners, PBL provides us with the ability to go off script from a traditionally developed lesson plan and develop the necessary support for everyone.

The required level of scaffolding for all learners is dependent on the needs of each individual. You might find your gifted learners need more scaffolding opportunities as they easily get lost in the minutia of specific requirements or are fearful of providing a "wrong" answer. Conversely, our traditionally labeled lower-level learners may need less direct support through the creation process and may only require modifications to reading materials or additional editing help. The key is to use your formative assessment records to inform your instruction at every stage of project assessment.

If all of the teachers in my department/school/district adopt a PBL approach, won't the technical experts in my community become overwhelmed with requests to help?

It is a good practice to build a database of potential community partners. If your school or district has a career counselor, start with the connections they have already developed and add to them. Within the database, I suggest you add a column to describe any project involvement from the partners. List the dates, type of involvement, and the teacher/school with whom the partner connected. A quick scan of the database will let you know if any one partner is tapped out for the marking period, semester, or year. However, large business partners also have more technical experts with whom you might connect.

Sometimes, all it takes is a cold call to one person from a potential business partner, and the message goes out to the entire company. One initial connection quickly turns into twenty. Thus, if you have a situation with multiple schools within the district implementing the same challenge at the same time, the likelihood that there are more than enough technical experts to go around is high. However, if you do run into logistical snags, think creatively about how you might get around the issue.

While you may be fortunate enough to find one technical expert who is willing to review ninety projects as I did, don't count on this possibility. Therefore, it may be that you turn an individual project into a team project to lessen the overall number of submissions. You might also think about choosing one overall class submission based on the feedback from your learners as to which is the best option. From this feedback, the entire class shifts their focus to the chosen best solution for the remainder of the project work. Furthermore, you may be able to slightly change the emphasis of the project generally from a local to a state, to a national viewpoint. For example, a local conservation district also has a state environmental counterpart, and if you are feeling ambitious, there is also the national possibility with the EPA.

I live in a very rural area, how will I connect with technical experts?

Similar to my response to the last question, you want to check with parents first to find out what they do for a living. You might be surprised at the options this presents you. Also, send out an all call to your staff to ask if they know anyone who has the special expertise that you are seeking. There may be an in-law or a neighbor that is a viable option.

Your next exploration should be via Nepris or Real World Scholars (discussed in Chapter 2). Both of these online options can connect from anywhere in the world and already have a database of experts. Finally, reach out on Twitter or LinkedIn if you feel comfortable; you never know who might respond.

If I don't teach on a block schedule, will PBL still work in my classroom?

The more time you have allotted during the day to dedicate to your PBL unit, the deeper your learners can dig into the inquiry questions they develop. A 47- to 53-minute period goes by very quickly compared to an 80- or 90-minute block. However, you can make whatever timeframe you have available work. Keep in mind that you will need to extend the number of days for shorter class duration to compensate for the lost time.

I've heard about schools that use a genius hour, can I use PBL during this time?

If you have a genius hour scheduled during your day, this is the perfect time to explore PBL. However, PBL should not solely live in this space and time. Often, learning experiences during genius hour end up becoming that research paper in disguise that I mentioned several times throughout this book. If you do decide to work within the confines of a genius hour, be sure to level up the learning experiences so that you meet the creation level of Bloom's. Otherwise, you may find that your learners don't take this time seriously.

I don't have much technology in my district, will PBL still work for me?

PBL was not an invented pedagogy for the introduction of computers in the classroom. I started my PBL approach long before I had access to a class set of laptops. I won't lie, however, technology access does make collaboration and communication more fluid for your learners. It also provides you with an easier way to track formative assessments. If you have limited access, this could become your authentic and relevant challenge. How can we increase technology access in our district?

I don't have a large budget for my classroom, how much does a PBL project cost to implement?

There is no reason that any PBL experience should cost money. You do not need a fancy 3D printer or a dedicated makerspace with all the bells and whistles. If, for some reason, your learners are attempting to install something on campus that does cost money, make that part of the learning experience. Inquiry is part of the challenge, and that process should dictate that your learners ask the hard questions on where they might gain access to the necessary funds. This need is also the perfect time to introduce a writing component to your challenge. The technical writing required for a grant proposal increases the complexity of the challenge. You may, in fact, want to partner with an ELA teacher for this portion of the experience.

State test scores are critical to our district's image, will PBL adequately prepare my learners to do well on these tests?

The majority of state test readiness, today, consists of a few weeks of preparation in the form of practice questions and last-minute lessons regarding frequently missed questions. Often, and the older our learners get, they dismiss the prep sessions. For those learners who have difficulty testing, the sessions merely increase their stress levels. For those learners who always do well, they can find the sessions mind-numbing. Of course, there are the learners in the middle of the pack who are mildly ambivalent toward the required practice.

Well-designed authentic challenges require our learners to go much deeper into the content and help them to develop better the skills included on these tests. Rather than complete a few assignments and activities during a traditionally crafted unit, our learners participate in a sustained inquiry process during the unit that enhances the mastery of standards and skills. While no direct test prep occurs during a PBL unit, our learners think at much higher levels and in a context that is relevant to them. These PBL experiences are a story of learning that ensures better retention of the experience, thus translating into automatic test preparation for our learners.

My administration wants me to inform my parents about PBL, how should I go about this?

I've worked with districts that decided to start a PBL campaign with letters home to parents and informational assemblies for the entire student body. There were PBL posters in every classroom, and every learner had a PBL notebook provided. I have even been flown in to sit on a panel for a one-hour meeting with parents to ease their angst about PBL. In short, these were mostly disasters that doomed these initiatives from the start.

Instead of thinking about PBL as something new, think about it as excellent instruction! Would you send home a letter or hold an assembly for any other pedagogical approach? If you make the shift to PBL without calling attention to it, there will be far less pushback. Instead, during an open house or back to school night, highlight the great learning experiences that you have planned. However, don't call them projects at this point, lest you scare off parents for their misunderstanding of what you intend.

I feel like I need to see this in action, what are the best "PBL" schools that I should model my program after?

I have to be brutally honest here: I don't think there is any one PBL model school that you should visit. Each set of schools has its own circumstances, community, and learners. While I believe learners are learners wherever you go, there are still nuances that we may not be aware of in any given situation. For example, one group of learners may have started in a PBL system from day one in kindergarten.

There are plenty of PBL school models that are out there, and some have bought into a system in which they pay a high price to be a member school. Without naming any of those, I'm sure you have researched a few of them. Some do PBL reasonably well, while others are merely PBL by name alone. Therefore, if you tailor a model to fit your needs, you will save money and also create an authentic, relevant, and appropriately complex ecosystem that isn't a replication but rather a designed solution to your personal challenge.

I'm still struggling to come up with a project idea, what are the best websites of projects for me to explore?

Do yourself a big favor and do not Google "PBL project ideas." More than likely, you will receive a return of lists that include everything and anything but what you seek. Below, however, is a list of websites that

I approve of for generating options that you could tailor to your own learners' pathways.

Project Invent:
www.projectinvent.org/projects

While this is a high school program, don't discount these ideas for your upper elementary and middle school learners. However, peruse the past projects to stimulate your creative thought process as you consider possible project ideas. Project Invent seeks to shift the concept of makerspaces from places to create "stuff" that is eventually thrown away to an environment that champions creativity to solve authentic problems.

Design Squad Global:
https://pbskids.org/designsquad/

PBS Kids runs a challenge idea every few months that you can join or just use as an idea starter for your classroom. There is also a section to peruse in which kids have submitted challenges they would like to see solved. Some of the kids' ideas are more difficult to envision than others such as walking on water, but others are more conceivable such as a recycling bin that can shred bottles and cans. At the very least, you can use this site to inspire creativity with your challenges!

Open IDEO:
https://challenges.openideo.com/challenge

Global challenges for social good are the specialty of this organization. However, don't think this is just a social studies teacher's dream. You can join an ongoing challenge or review past challenges to garner ideas on how your content and curriculum connects to the real world. Direct participation on Open IDEO has a few phases that allow for ideation, iteration, feedback, and implementation.

Global Youth Debates:
www.globalyouthdebates.com/debate-topic.html

This site has debate formats and protocols that may interest some of you, but it's the themes that may spark an idea for an authentic challenge. You will need to take the topic statement and turn it into a launch question, however.

Appendix 1
A Guide to Tools, Activities, and Protocols

All of the tools, activities, and protocols shared here are designed to work with any grade level and any content area. Make adjustments as needed and as appropriate for your learners. Some of these tools were discussed in more detail, in the context of a project, in the preceding chapters. All of the tools are listed in alphabetical order and are not ranked according to any preference. This is meant to be a quick reference guide for your planning purposes. This list was published initially in Laur and Ackers (2017) and has been modified and expanded here.

3-2-1 Reflection

- Exit ticket reflection strategy
- List three things learned
- List two things found interesting
- List one question you still have

3-12-3 Brainstorm

- Three minutes to brainstorm general ideas about the topic – individuals in the group write ideas on index cards
- Twelve minutes to combine ideas into a rough concept – pair off and draw three index cards to shape thinking
- Three minutes to share rough concept with the group

Agreement Circles

- Arrange learners in a circle
- Provide a statement for the class to consider
- All learners who agree with the statement move to the center of the circle
- Match learners up to form pairs between an agreer and a non-agreer
- Discuss for a few minutes

- Ask learners to move their position if their initial thoughts have changed
- Share out as a class

Anchor Charts

- Anchor charts make thinking and processes visible
- As you uncover new strategies, processes, cues, guidelines, and other content create a chart to visually represent the learning
- You may have multiple anchor charts positioned around the room related to any given challenge

Brain Drain

- Create groups of six
- Provide an empty 3 × 6 grid so that each learner has an empty row
- At the top of the grid, list three prompts for brainstorming purposes
- Each learner brainstorms potential ideas in their row for each of the prompts
- Pass papers so that other learners may add ideas to their assigned row without duplicating responses (or complete online as a simultaneous dump of ideas)

Café Conversations (The World Café)

- Small group conversations with provided question stems
- Three rounds lasting 5 to 7 minutes each
- Chart paper at each table to write, doodle, and draw
- Table host stays put while others travel to new conversations with new ideas, themes, and questions

Circle Square Triangle Reflection

- Exit ticket reflection strategy
- Draw a triangle and list three important points from the day or the reading
- Draw a square and write down anything that they agree or are "square" with
- Draw a circle and write down any question they might still have or that is "circling" in their mind

♦ Note: This is a good opportunity to talk about "being square" with a concept and having a question that is "circling" in their mind

Consequence and Sequel

- ♦ Based on the premise that a new invention, plan, rule, or decision has consequences that go on for a long time
- ♦ Learners consider the immediate, short-term, medium-term, and long-term consequences of an action (make time adaptations as appropriate for younger learners, as they can't focus as far into the future)
- ♦ Others often see the consequences of your solution when you do not

Co-op Strip Paragraphs (GLAD)

- ♦ Provide a topic sentence – GLAD uses one created via the Process Grid activity
- ♦ Every child or every group is responsible for adding a sentence to the original
- ♦ The class or small group reads the co-created paragraph, together

Dot Voting

- ♦ Create a master list of all learner-generated ideas and display on chart paper
- ♦ Provide each learner with a given quantity of dot stickers (2–5 depending on how many total topics you wish to generate)
- ♦ Learners quietly vote by placing a sticker next to the topic(s) they prefer

Experts in the House

- ♦ Create an expert group based on the Process Grid
- ♦ Much like a jigsaw method, choose one learner from each group to represent a concept
- ♦ Expert groups research information
- ♦ Expert groups share information with the class or with their original groups
- ♦ Note: This can be done as an online or analog version

Feedback Carousel (National School Reform Faculty)

- Display the main components of your idea on a piece of chart paper and hang on a wall or lay on a table
- Divide a second sheet of chart paper into four quadrants: clarifying questions, probing questions, recommendations, and resources
- Learners walk around the room and provide feedback
- Sticky notes are used to place the feedback in the appropriate quadrant

Frayer Model/Four Box Vocabulary

- Create a diagram that is similar to the Reframing Matrix
- Use the center of the diagram to list the vocabulary word
- Use each of the four segmented portions of the rectangle to list each of the following:
    - Definition
    - Examples
    - Non-examples
    - Illustration of the vocabulary word

GRASPS

- Identify the real-world connection to each of the following:
    - Goal
    - Role
    - Audience
    - Situation
    - Product/Performance
    - Standards

Guided Reciprocal Teaching or Peer Teaching

- Learners take on the roles and lead their own discussions
- Roles to include:
    - Questioning
    - Clarifying
    - Summarizing
    - Predicting

I Know/You Know (Literacy TA)

- Structured Pair Share
- Partner A shares for 30 seconds. Partner B actively listens, takes notes
- Partner B summarizes what Partner A shared for 30 seconds
- Partner A shares for 30 seconds. Partner B actively listens, takes notes
- Partner B summarizes what Partner A shared for 30 seconds
- Find new partners, repeat four times

Inside Outside Circles (Kagan)

- Form two circles of learners with one circle literally inside of the other
- Partner learners with one from the inside circle and the other from the outside circle
- Partner A summarizes the information from the story or lesson (timed)
- Partner B listens and then adds to the summary (timed)
- Move the outside circle round by two people
- New partners repeat the process
- The teacher listens from the center of the two circles

Interactive Journal

- Graphically Organized Reading Notes
- Encourage developmentally appropriate independent writing

Mind Maps

- Represent the main idea through an image or chosen word
- Create branches to represent pictures or words related to the main idea
- Connect additional sub-branches that extend ideas and thinking

Invented Dialogs

- Weave together real quotes from primary sources to match the context of the discussion

Observation Chart (GLAD)

- Provide color photos of the topic on poster paper
- Groups of learners are given one marker only and, as a group, write
  - An observation
  - A question
  - A comment

Open-Narrow-Close

- Open Phase: Generate as many ideas as possible
- Narrow Phase: Clarify, categorize, and prioritize possible solutions
- Close Phase: Select a final solution to implement

Pass Around Strategy

- Learners work in cooperative writing groups to develop a variety of possible stories around a single prompt

Pass the Problem

- Groups are given a variety of case studies/problems
- Write down the first step in analyzing the problem
- Pass the problem to the next group to add the second step in analyzing the problem
- Continue until all groups have added their thoughts
- Note: The added challenge is in the number of groups (3, 4, 5, 6 steps) to get to the solution. Therefore, it is okay if a group notices a gap in the solution process and goes back to add a step in between two that are listed

Pinwheel Discussion

- Divide class into four groups with "speaker" seats arranged as a square facing each other
- Seats behind the speaker are arranged as a triangle: two behind, three behind the two, four behind the three, etc.
- Three groups are given a specific point of view to represent
- Fourth group is designated as the "challengers"
- Groups prepare together and then rotate positions to allow for a new speaker every few minutes

Problem Breakdown

- Write the challenge question at the top of a piece of chart paper
- List or breakdown every part of the problem
- Turn each part of the problem into a question
- Use the questions to begin to gather information, research, and data as part of the inquiry process

Process Grid (GLAD)

- Categorize concepts from the project
- Use the concept and the categories to create a grid of related and unrelated ideas
- Learners collaboratively fill in the grid with important information

Quiz-Quiz-Trade

- Peer review of information by asking and answering questions to think about solutions
- Learners are given a question to solve and then they find a partner to quiz and vice versa
- Once finished, they break off and find new partners

Random Pictures Story

- Provide groups with a series of seemingly unrelated pictures (check out discarded magazines from the library to find some great ones)
- Ask groups to create a story out of the pictures as it relates to the challenge they have been given
- Note: The same pictures could be used for any challenge with very different meanings and contexts as they relate to the challenge

Ranking Alternatives

- Given a challenge, learners list as many possible solutions as they can in a timed period (determine this number based on the challenge and grade level of your class)
- Rank the compiled list of solutions in order of preference
- This can lead into a **Dot Voting** activity

Reflective Central Idea Diagram

- Central or main idea in the center with lines radiating from center
- Each line connects to a new box
- Each box contains a question: Where did we start? Where are we now? Where are we going?
- Reflective diagramming assists a learner in synthesizing information based on investigations and designs

Reframing Matrix

- Create a four-box grid with the problem or challenge listed in the center
- Use the 4Ps to fill in the boxes with the following perspectives:
  - People
  - Product
  - Planning
  - Potential

Reversal Technique

- Identify the problem or challenge
- Reverse the problem – "How could I possibly cause the problem?"
- Brainstorm to generate reverse solution ideas
- Evaluate these solution ideas and how they help to see the original problem in a new light

Roving Reporter

- One team member moves around the room to gather information
- Report back to their team any ideas that might be useful

Say Something

- Find an appropriate text and break the text into chunks
- At each chunk, have pairs of learners stop and "Say Something" related to what they just read
- If one partner finishes reading a section before the other, they sit quietly and process what they have read
- This can be done as an oral activity, recorded activity, or completed with a written online transcript of the conversation

SCAMPER

- A mnemonic that stands for substitute, combine, adapt, modify, put to another use, eliminate, and reverse
- Use the words to create specific questions as solutions to challenges are considered

Snowball Discussion

- Start with a discussion prompt for pairs of learners to discuss
- After approximately 3 minutes, two pairs join for a group of four to expand the discussion
- Now, groups of four join another group of four and continue the discussion (monitor your times based on auditory cues from the discussion waning)
- This process continues until the entire class is engaged in one discussion

Socratic Seminar

- Arrange learners in a circle
- Ask a guiding question for the discussion
- Have learners respond to the question in a discussion format, but encourage them to ask questions during the discussion
- Every time someone asks a question, clap your hands and record the question
- At the conclusion of the discussion, affinity map the questions
  - Have your learners determine three categories for the questions
  - Categorize the questions into the categories
  - Use the categories of questions to take the next steps in the project
- Note: This is my version of this popular discussion approach

Sound Bite

- Groups must create an elevator pitch of their ideas using only 27 words, in 9 seconds, with 3 thoughts

Space Method

- *Summary*: Today I learned ... The main idea(s) ...

- *Process*: As I recorded information, I thought about ... I was challenged today because ...
- *Analyze*: _____ (topic) consist of ... X and Y are critical concepts ...
- *Connect*: While learning about _____, I thought of ... Topic X is similar to ...
- *Evaluate*: Today was helpful because ... It's important to understand ...

Spider Web Discussion

- Place learners in a circle
- Provide a discussion prompt or question
- Use chart paper to identify where learners sit in the circle
- As learners participate in the discussion, map the conversation by drawing lines between each learner as they talk
- The end result should look like a spider web
- This is loosely based on the Harkness Discussion Protocol with a few modifications
- I like to give bonus participation to our learners who take the conversation to the next level by asking a deep question or appropriately challenging a comment made by a peer
- You can do this as a pass/fail activity – everyone must participate to pass or everyone fails
- Everyone learns communication skills as they figure out how to skillfully draw individuals into a conversation

Start, Stop, Continue

- Team reflection process
- Individuals determine and share out the following:
  - What they want to start doing
  - What they want to stop doing
  - What they want to continue doing

Story Maps

- Use a story that has a clear problem and a defined outcome
- List the problem, the characters, the events that took place leading up to the solution, and the final solution

SWOT Analysis (Good, Grow, Possible, Buggy – use for upper elementary)

- What are the strengths, weaknesses, opportunities, and threats to a possible solution?
- Look at these from both an internal and external frame of reference (things we can control and things we can't)

Text Clue Conclusion Groups

- Read a text
- Identify personal connections to the text
- Learners map or the teacher maps personal connections
- Look for patterns
- Connect patterns to a challenge or issue

Think It Through

- Role-play real-life scenarios
- Use cause and effect to discuss consequences and that consequences affect others

Things You Know

- Have groups who are assigned a topic create envelopes with strips of paper inside that include pieces of information that other learners should already know about and things they need to investigate more
- This facilitates a jigsaw approach to topics of investigation

Thousand Word Pictures

- Learners take digital pictures they believe express their understanding of a topic
- Alternatively, learners can write 1,000 words to express their understanding

Three-Step Interview

- Work in pairs to interview each other (steps one and two)
- Take turns sharing information to the entire group (step three)

To Be or Not to Be Protocol

- Peer partners share the biggest problem encountered with the identified solution
- Feedback
- Reflection

Upside Down Gallery Walk

- Teams or individual learners display their work on a large poster
- Teams or individual learners analyze posters and provide feedback on a sticky note
- All feedback is written on the sticky side and then the sticky note is placed on the poster so that no one is able to read the feedback until the end of the walk

Word of the Day/Week

- Choose a word (or several words) on which to focus for the class period or the whole week
- Encourage learners to include the word(s) as frequently as possible in the appropriate context of their conversations in pairs, small groups, or as a whole class

Yarn–Yarn

- The structure provides a record of interaction patterns
- Each time a team member wants to talk, he/she must wrap the yarn around his/her finger
- At the end of the conversation, the visual should provide information for reflection on who did the most/least amount of talking

Appendix 2
Templates and Tools

The following pages are templates and planning tools to support you as you develop your scaffolds for your learners through a project-based design approach to instruction.

This table is a space to plan your authentic learning experience. Here, brainstorm notes, ideas, and possible scaffolds to include in your challenge design. Remember to use the question at each stage to guide you in this development process.

Stages of Project Assessment	
Stage 1: Challenge and Purpose	
How do we know if our learners understand and are invested in the challenge?	
Stage 2: Inquiry and Ideas	
How do we know if our learners have explored multiple pathways to a solution?	
Stage 3: Context and Perspective	
How do we know if our learners have considered end-user needs and technical expert feedback?	
Stage 4: Actions and Consequences	
How do we know if our learners have considered the potential positive and negative impacts of their proposed solution?	
Stage 5: Options and Opportunities	
How do we know if our learners have an actionable solution for their intended end-users?	

Bloom's Taxonomy: Scaffold Your Questions	
Create	
Evaluate	
Analyze	
Apply	
Understand	
Remember	

Appendix 3
Suggested Options for Authentic Challenge Questions

These are suggested options for authentic challenge questions from the community-based project ideas in Chapter 1, Table 1.4. While there is no one right answer, please remember the elements of writing a good project challenge.

Community Assets	Authentic Challenge Question
Airport	1. How can we make the future of air travel safer for passengers? 2. How can we attract new airline routes and discount carriers to our regional airport?
Chamber of Commerce	1. How can we restore vibrancy in our city to combat economic decline? 2. How can we redevelop an abandoned property to attract businesses to our community?
Conservation District	1. How can we design a plan for the conservation of farmland in our community to protect family farms in the future? 2. How can we create an efficient crop irrigation system while simultaneously conserving our water resources?
Department of Transportation	1. How can we redesign the traffic patterns to protect walkers in our area? 2. How can we attract an affordable public transportation system that will meet the needs of our community for the next twenty-five years?
Public Library	1. How can we design an app that provides virtual services to our library community while ensuring we still meet their needs in our physical building? 2. How can we convince the state government to increase the funding for our local library?

Bibliography

American Poetry and Literacy Program, Ed. (2006). *How to eat a poem: A smorgasbord of tasty and delicious poems for young readers.* Mineola, NY: Dover Publications.

Angelo, T. & Cross, P. (1993). *Classroom assessment techniques.* San Francisco, CA: Jossey-Bass.

Armstrong, K., Parmelee, M., Santifort, S., Burley, J., van Fleet, J.W., Koziol, M., et al. (2018). *Preparing tomorrow's workforce for the Fourth Industrial Revolution: An executive summary.* London, UK: Deloitte.

Backchannel Chat. (2019). Retrieved from http://backchannelchat.com

Chaltain, S. (2011). *Faces of learning: 50 powerful stories of defining moments in education.* San Francisco, CA: Jossey-Bass.

Cort Learning. (n.d.). Consequence and Sequel. Retrieved from www.cortthinking.net/files/student-pdfs/CoRT1/CoRT1_4.pdf

Cuban, M., Patel, S. & McCue, I. (2018). *Kid start-up: How you can be an entrepreneur.* New York, NY: Diversion Books.

de Ruijter, R. (n.d.). Reversal – Change your perspective and solve your problem. Retrieved from https://hatrabbits.com/en/reversal/

Dean, C. & Kato, A. (2008). *Girlwood.* New York, NY: Houghton Mifflin.

Delany, M. (2000). *Misfits Inc. No. 4: The kingfisher's tale.* Atlanta, GA: Peachtree Publishers.

Deloitte Global & Global Business Coalition for Education. (2018). Preparing tomorrow's workforce for the Fourth Industrial Revolution – Executive summary. Retrieved from https://www2.deloitte.com/global/en/pages/about-deloitte/articles/gx-preparing-tomorrow-workforce-for-the-fourth-industrial-revolution.html

Design Squad Global. (2019). Retrieved from https://pbskids.org/designsquad

Diigo. (2019). Retrieved from www.diigo.com/

Draper, S.M. (2012). *Out of my mind.* New York, NY: Atheneum Books for Young Readers.

Eamer, C. & Edlund, B. (2017). *What a waste! Where does garbage go?* Toronto, ON: Annick Press.

Eliot, M. (2016). *Kid millionaire: Over 50 exciting business ideas.* Kennebunkport, ME: Applesauce Press.

Equity Maps. (2019). Retrieved from www.equitymaps.com

Expeditionary Learning. (n.d.). Say something protocol. Retrieved from www.moboces.org/UserFiles/Servers/Server_917767/File/Programs%20&%20Services/Professional%20Development/PBL/22%20Say%20Something.pdf

Fixperts. (2019). Retrieved from http://fixing.education/fixperts

Gamestorming. (n.d.a). 3-12-3 Brainstorm. Retrieved from http://gamestorming.com/games-for-design/3-12-3-brainstorm/

Gamestorming. (n.d.b). NUF test. Retrieved from https://gamestorming.com/nuf-test/

Global Youth Debates. (2019). www.globalyouthdebates.com/debate-topic.html

Google Tour Creator. (2019). Retrieved from https://vr.google.com/tourcreator/

Graff, G. & Birkenstein, C. (2012). *"They say/I say": The moves that matter in academic writing, with readings*. New York, NY: W.W. Norton & Co.

Hamilton, E., Rosenberg, J. & Akcaoglu, M. (2016). The substitution augmentation modification redefinition (SAMR) model: A critical review and suggestions for its use. *Tech Trends*, 60(5), 433–441.

Hyde, C.R. (2014). *Pay it forward (young reader's edition)*. New York, NY: Simon & Schuster.

ISTE. (n.d.). ISTE standards for students. Retrieved from www.iste.org/standards/for-students

Janeczko, P. (2015). *The death of a hat: A brief history of poetry in fifty objects*. Somerville, MA: Candlewick Press.

Kagan. (n.d.). Three-step interview process. Retrieved from http://et.nwresd.org/files/Three_Step_Interview.pdf

Kagan Strategies. (n.d.). Inside outside circles. Retrieved from https://wvde.state.wv.us/strategybank/Inside-OutsideCircle.html

Kaizena. (2019). Retrieved from www.kaizena.com

Laur, D. (2013). *Authentic learning experiences: A real-world approach to project-based learning*. New York, NY: Routledge.

Laur, D. & Ackers, J. (2017). *Developing natural curiosity through project-based learning: Five strategies for the PreK-3 classroom*. New York, NY: Routledge.

Lexipedia. (2019). Retrieved from www.lexipedia.com/

Literacy, T.A. (n.d.). I know/you know. Retrieved from www.literacyta.com/literacy-skills/i-know-you-know

Lowry, L. (1993). *The giver*. New York, NY: Laurel Leaf Books.

Mentimeter. (2019). Retrieved from www.mentimeter.com

Microsoft. (2018). Microsoft artificial intelligence commercial. Retrieved from www.youtube.com/watch?v=7rzufxlGH4o

Mind Tools. (n.d.a). Reframing matrix. Retrieved from www.mindtools.com/pages/article/newCT_05.htm

Mind Tools. (n.d.b). SCAMPER. Retrieved from www.mindtools.com/pages/article/newCT_02.htm

National Council for the Social Studies. (2013). *The college, career, and civic life (C3) framework for social studies state standards: Guidance for enhancing the rigor of K-12 civics, economics, geography, and history.* Silver Spring, MD: NCSS.

National Governor's Association for Best Practices, Council of Chief State Officers. (2010). *Common core state standards initiative.* Washington, DC: National Governor's Association for Best Practices, Council of Chief State Officers.

National School Reform Faculty. (n.d.a). Back to the future. Retrieved from www.nsrfharmony.org/wp-content/uploads/2017/10/future.pdf

National School Reform Faculty. (n.d.b). Feedback carousel. Retrieved from www.nsrfharmony.org/system/files/protocols/feed_back_carousel.pdf

National School Reform Faculty. (n.d.c). Three levels of text protocol. Retrieved from www.nsrfharmony.org/wp-content/uploads/2017/10/3_levels_text_0.pdf

Nepris. (2019). Retrieved from www.nepris.com/

NewsMap. (2019). Retrieved from http://newsmap.jp

NGSS Lead States. (2013). *Next generation science standards: For states, by states.* Washington, DC: The National Academies Press.

Notability. (2019). Retrieved from www.gingerlabs.com

One Stone. (2018). Our pitch was perfect. Well, almost … Retrieved from https://onestone.org/one-stone-voice/2018/6/12/our-pitch-was-perfect-well-almost

Open IDEO. (2019). Retrieved from https://challenges.openideo.com/challenge

Project GLAD. (n.d.). Orange County Department of Education. Retrieved from http://projectgladstudy.educationnorthwest.org/what-is-glad

Project Invent. (2019). Retrieved from http://projectinvent.org/projects

Real World Scholars. (2019). Retrieved from www.realworldscholars.org/

Ring, S. (2005). *Helping hands.* Minneapolis, MN: Capstone Publishing.

Rothstein, D. & Santana, L. (2011). *Make just one change: Teach students to ask their own questions.* Cambridge, MA: Harvard Education Press.

Sachar, L. (2015). *Fuzzy mud.* New York, NY: Random House.

SAP Roambi. (n.d.). Retrieved from www.sap.com/products/roambi.html

Schwab, K. (2016). *The fourth industrial revolution.* New York, NY: Crown Business.

Scrumy. (2019). Retrieved from scrumy.com

Snelling, J. (2018). New ISTE standards aim to develop lifelong learners. Retrieved from www.iste.org/explore/ISTE-blog/New-ISTE-standards-aim-to-develop-lifelong-learners

Solheim, J. & Brace, E. (2001). *It's disgusting and we ate it! True food facts from around the world and throughout history.* New York, NY: Simon & Schuster.

Sundem, G. (2010). *Real kids, real stories, real change: Courageous actions around the world.* Minneapolis, MN: Free Spirit Publishing.

United States Department of Education. (n.d.). Family Educational Rights and Privacy Act. Retrieved from www2.ed.gov/policy/gen/guid/fpco/ferpa/index.html

Virginia Department of Education. (2015). Health standards of learning. Retrieved from www.doe.virginia.gov/testing/sol/standards_docs/health/index.shtml

VoiceThread. (2019). Retrieved from https://voicethread.com

WebJets. (2019). Retrieved from www.webjets.io

weFlipGrid. (2019). Retrieved from https://flipgrid.com

Wiggins, G. & McTighe, J. (2004). *Understanding by design professional development workbook.* Alexandria, VA: Association for Supervision and Curriculum Development.

For Product Safety Concerns and Information please contact our EU
representative GPSR@taylorandfrancis.com
Taylor & Francis Verlag GmbH, Kaufingerstraße 24, 80331 München, Germany

www.ingramcontent.com/pod-product-compliance
Lightning Source LLC
Chambersburg PA
CBHW080938300426
44115CB00017B/2876